What's With Those
ADIRONDACK
MOUNTAIN NAMES?

Seneca Ray Stoddard's map of the ADIRONDACKS,
Courtesy of Adirondack Research Library

What's With Those
ADIRONDACK
MOUNTAIN NAMES?

Buck,

Enjoy each mountain's
story.

Bob Lawrence

WRITTEN AND COMPILED BY

Robert C. Lawrence

COVER IMAGE — Blue Mountain and Fall Foliage Reflected in Lake Durant
photo by Mark Bowie (Front Cover)

BOOK DESIGN — The Troy Book Makers | Meradith Kill

Printed in the United States of America

The Troy Book Makers • Troy, New York • thetroybookmakers.com

To order additional copies of this title, contact your favorite local bookstore
or visit www.shoptbmbooks.com

Library of Congress Control Number: 2021915084
ISBN: 978-1-61468-652-1

To my wife, **Carol Ann,**
who sparked my interest in
Adirondack Mountain place names
and accompanied me throughout this journey.

CONTENTS

ACKNOWLEDGMENTS

This book required a great deal of research and personal contact to seek answers, and I want to thank all of those who helped and supported me through this journey.

I want to thank my wife, Carol Ann, for being a catalyst in this endeavor and her support, patience, suggestions, insight, and encouragement over the past six years.

From the beginning and throughout this inquiry, Margie Amodeo, Kelly Adirondack Center Coordinator, helped me seek information on specific mountain place names. She also permitted me to utilize the Adirondack Research Library's massive collection of resources, including rare books, documents, maps, photographs, and primary documents.

The Kelly Adirondack Center, located in conservationist and Adirondack author Paul Schaefer's former home in Niskayuna, is operated by Union College, Schenectady, New York. The center not only houses the research library but offers many exemplary programs on the Adirondacks for students of Union and the public.

A very special thank you to those who spent many hours proofreading and editing the book: Rich and Diane Dixson, Elizabeth and Gary Garavuso, and Elaine Asselin.

I want to thank Dale Wade-Keszey for writing the song "What's With Those Names" for the book.

Many other people contributed to this project. Thank you to the following: Karen Peters, Guy Stephenson, and Doug Wolfe, Wilmington Historical Society; Mike Lynch, multimedia reporter, *Adirondack Explorer*; Debra Kimok, librarian, Special Collections, Feinberg Library, S.U.N.Y. Plattsburgh; Jane Bouchard and Laura Dewey, Schroon Lake Public Library; Roberta Games, Hadley-Lake Luzerne Historical Society; Catherine Moore and Joe Hackett, *Adirondack Daily Enterprise*; Tony Goodwin, author, and guide; Lawrence Gooley, author; Erik Schlimmer, author; Ivy Gocker, library director, Adirondack Experience; Michele Tucker, curator, Adirondack Research Room, Saranac Lake Free Library; Havidan Rodriguez, president and Michael Christakis, vice president of student affairs, University at Albany, New York; Casey Crandall, Justin, and Heidi LaPrairie, Dippikill Wilderness Retreat; Margaret Mannix, Lake George historian; William Zullo, former Hamilton County historian; and Matthew Golebiewski, project archivist, Schaffer Library, Union College.

Also, a warm thank you to Gary Garavuso, McKenzie Cantwell Jones, Michael and Colleen Meyer, Dick Tucker, and Dale and Joan Wade-Keszey, who encouraged me and provided valuable assistance.

And finally, Meradith Kill (author liaison/graphic designer/eBookologist) of The Troy Book Makers, you were a pleasure to work with, and I want to sincerely thank you for all your help. Everything was done very professionally, in a timely manner, and always including me in the process. I could not be happier with how you transformed my manuscript and formatted it into a skillfully designed book.

FOREWORD

It was a beautiful June day on a peaceful, calm Lake Durant, located not far from the hamlet of Blue Mountain Lake. Schools were not yet out for the summer, so the adjacent Lake Durant State Campground (William W. Durant, builder of Adirondack Great Camps) was empty. A pair of adult and young loons put a show on for my wife and me as we sat in our kayaks. While observing these majestic Adirondack icons, we noticed Blue Mountain looming above us. Knowing that I have both a degree and a self-taught background in history, my wife, Carol Ann, asked, "Where does Blue Mountain get its name?" I told her I did not know the answer and suggested we drive to the Adirondack Museum at Blue Mountain Lake (now the Adirondack Experience) the following day to buy a book on regional place names.

The next day we went to the museum and found nothing on this subject. Thus, I began my quest to research place names for Blue Mountain and other Adirondack Park peaks. There are hundreds of mountains, so I had to limit my study. I settled on the hundred highest, the Saranac Six, the Tupper Lake Triad, and some personal-choice peaks.

As I continued, I learned that I was studying toponymy, a geographic term for studying human and natural place names such as cities, countries, rivers, and mountains. The word comes from the Greek topos for "place" and onoma for a "name." Those places are called toponyms, and a mountain place name is an oronym.

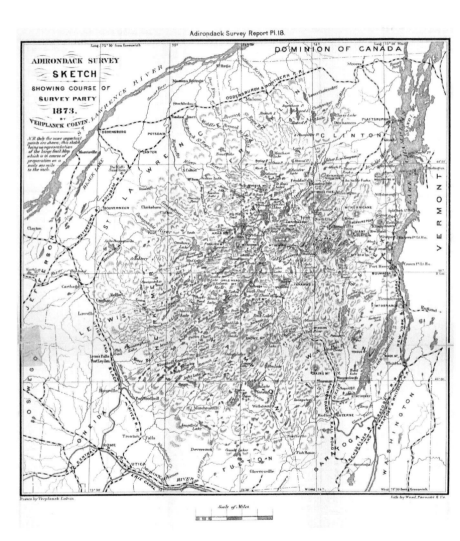

1873 ADIRONDACK SURVEY SKETCH by Verplanck Colvin,
Courtesy of Adirondack Research Library

INTRODUCTION

The first people to give names to the Adirondack mountains were the Algonquin and Iroquois native people who hunted in the Adirondacks. Very few of the place names they coined still exist today. Early settlers left their names on mountains too.

Many mountains were named or renamed by others as they traveled through and studied the area. One of the first explorers in the Adirondacks in 1836 was Ebenezer Emmons, a scientist. He was appointed State Geologist for the Northern New York Geological District by the then-sitting Governor of New York State, William Learned Marcy. Along with scientists, Emmons made the first ascent of what they later named Mount Marcy, the highest mountain in the area, after Governor Marcy. Emmons named this northern area of New York State the Adirondacks and would name other mountains in the region.

The one person most responsible for naming many Adirondack mountains was Verplanck Colvin, an Albany native who conducted "The Adirondack Survey." The New York State Legislature commissioned the Adirondack Survey to explore and survey the Adirondacks. Accompanying and helping with this survey was a group of guides who lived in these mountains and many scientists from various fields of study. One of the most famous Adirondack guides was Orson Schofield (Old Mountain) Phelps. He and the Colvin crew members named many of the peaks.

Animals, shapes, water bodies, famous, and not-so-famous people have their names depicted on the Adirondack Mountains. It is a long process for a mountain to be named for a person. Briefly, first, a person has to have been deceased for several years before the process to name or rename the mountain can begin. Then, after local and state people advocate for the name, it goes to the New York State Committee on Geographic Names. If accepted, it next has to be approved by the United States Board on Geographic Names, a Geological Survey branch. Finally, the mountain name is made official. The most recent woman who went through this process was Inez Milholland. Mount Discovery was changed to Mount Inez, located in Essex County in the town of Lewis.

Following the Acknowledgments, Foreword, Introduction, song lyrics- "What's With Those Names," and The Adirondacks, this book is arranged by chapters in alphabetical order. The first chapter is "A- Oronyms." and so forth. The chapters' entries are in alphabetical order. Following the Oronym chapters are Notes and Bibliography.

Each lettered oronym chapter lists its entries in alphabetical order according to their official name and elevation by the 2021 United States Geological Survey. Such entries may appear as a mountain (ex. Fishing Brook Mountain), as a peak (ex. Averill Peak), as a mount (ex. Mount Marcy), as a ridge (ex. Rocky Peak Ridge), or by nothing but the mountain name (ex. Gothics). Mount, peak, and ridge are synonyms for mountain. Each entry also includes the special group it belongs to as well as its location (region, county, and town).

Below is a list of abbreviations found in each entry.

- **U.S.G.S.** — United States Geological Society
- **H.H.** — Hundred Highest mountains (based on a list from www.adirondack-park.net/peaks)
- **S.S.** — Saranac Six
- **T.L.T.** — Tupper Lake Triad
- **ft.** — feet
- **F.T.** — Fire Tower, still in existence today and opened to the public.

WHAT'S WITH THOSE NAMES

BY SINGER-SONGWRITER, Dale Wade-Keszey

What's with those names
Do they tell who went before us
And frame our rocks and forests
Or measure some acclaim

And who was there
When all the names were given
Were they long dead or still living
When they received immortal fame
Through those names

What's with those names
Was there any rhyme or reason
Did they have some special meaning
Or did someone just proclaim
And pick those names

Are those mountains really blue
Or do they seem grayer to you
Does the wind like a giant roar
A panther roam that forest floor
Did a Hadley live near by
What did Prospect Mt. hide

What's with those names
We visit through the seasons
We find it all so damn pleasing
But could someone please explain
What's with those names

Can a mountain be table flat
Pretty high for some hay to be stacked

Hurricane must have blown on through
An avalanche must happen too
Marcy was some important guy
But the rest can you tell me why

What's with those names
Guess I could live without knowing
It sure won't stop me from going
But could you throw a bone my way
What's with those names

THE ADIRONDACKS

Across from Lake Durant (Hamilton County) is a New York State Historical Marker. The New York State Education Department and Department of Public Works erected the marker in 1967. It is entitled "Historic New York: The Adirondacks."

The inscription reads as follows:

"The Adirondack Mountains, consisting of rocky peaks, sheer cliffs, and narrow valleys, also have wooded slopes and sparkling lakes. Forty-three mountains have elevations 4000 feet or higher. Mount Marcy, with an altitude of 5344 feet, is the highest. Near Marcy's summit is Lake Tear-of-the-Clouds, the source of the Hudson River.

Iroquois Indians derisively gave the name Adirondack (meaning "tree-eater") to some of the Algonkians, their enemies. In the early Adirondack history, Native Americans used the area for hunting. White men did not arrive on the scene until the late 18th century. Mining began at the end of that century, and Adirondack mines have yielded such ores as iron, zinc, titanium, talc, and garnet. The great wealth of Adirondack forests supplied timber demands in the nineteenth century and the first decades of the 20th. Alarmed over the denuding of this natural treasure, New York set up the Forest Preserve in 1885. The Adirondack Park now consists of more than two million State-owned acres.

Railroad construction after 1871 turned remote forest retreats into popular summer resorts. The opening of automobile highways in the 20th century made the area accessible for all to enjoy the rugged beauty of the Adirondack Mountains."[1]

The Adirondack Park today encompasses more than six million acres of land. Yellowstone, the Grand Canyon, Yosemite, and Glacier National Parks could fit inside the Adirondack Park confines. Unlike the national parks, the Adirondack Park or Adirondacks state-owned and public land have no kiosks charging entry fees. It is the largest public park in the lower forty-eight states.

---

1   ___ "Historic New York: The Adirondacks." *The Historical Marker Database*. Accessed April 24, 2019. https://www. hmdb.org/marker.asp?marker=44686.

A-ORONYMS

*"The mountains are calling & and I must go &
I will work on while I can, studying incessantly."*

—— JOHN MUIR ——

1873, Naturalist
(letter to his sister, Sarah Muir Galloway)

Without VERPLANCK COLVIN there would
be no Adirondack Park

Courtesy of Adirondack Research Library

MOUNT ADAMS

U.S.G.S. ELEVATION 3520 ft. (H.H.) F.T.

High Peaks Region, Essex County, Town of Newcomb

Mount Adams was initially called Mount Robinson to honor Archibald Robinson, said to have been an early mine executive. However, Verplanck Colvin changed the name to Mount Adams for someone well-known in the area. He stated in his *Report on the Topographical Survey of the Adirondack Wilderness of New York, for the Year 1873* that "the appropriateness of the new names of Mt. Redfield, Mt. Street and Mt. Adams given to summits hitherto unnamed will be appreciated by those acquainted with the written history of the area."[2] Mr. Adams could have been a landowner, a businessman, or a local politician.

Mount Adams had another distinction. On July 15, 1932, Adirondack Preservationist Paul Schaefer met Bob Marshall, an American forester, wilderness advocate, and writer. While they were standing on Mount Marcy's summit, Paul pointed out to Bob the lumbering going on Mount Adams. Being a forester and preservationist, Bob Marshall was quite upset about this destruction of the forests. He said, "We simply must band together—all of us who love

---

2   Verplanck Colvin. *Report on the Topographical Survey of the Adirondack Wilderness of New York, for the Year 1873.* (Albany, NY: Weed, Parsons & Company Printers, 1874).

the wilderness. We must fight together—wherever and whenever wilderness is attacked. We must mobilize all of our resources, all of our energies, all of our devotion to the wilderness. To fail to do this is to permit the American wilderness to be destroyed."[3] The people Marshall banded together formed the Wilderness Society.

ALGONQUIN PEAK
U.S.G.S. ELEVATION 5105 ft. (H.H.)
High Peaks Region, Essex County, Town of North Elba

This second highest peak in the Adirondacks, Algonquin, was initially named Mount McIntyre for Archibald McIntyre, the McIntyre Iron Works owner in nearby Tahawus by Ebeneezer Emmons. Ebeneezer Emmons, David Henderson, Archibald McIntyre, William Redfield, John Cheney, and others climbed Algonquin three days after Mount Marcy. Archibald McIntyre also served in New York State as a state comptroller, a state assembly, and senate member in later years.

About 1880, Verplanck Colvin renamed it Mount Algonquin for the Native Americans who hunted and fished in the Adirondacks but lived on its outskirts. In the United States Geological Survey, it is called Algonquin Peak.

3   Margaret (Margie) Amodeo, Hallie Bond, Carl George, J. Douglas Klein, and Richard E. Tucker. *The Adirondack Chronology.* Accessed February 9, 2020. https://digitalworks.union.edu/cgi/viewcontent. cgi?article=1000&context=arlpublications, 143.

ALLEN MOUNTAIN

U.S.G.S. ELEVATION 4321 ft. (H.H.)

High Peaks Region, Essex County, Town of Keene

Frederick Baylies Allen was an Episcopal minister in Boston and a pioneer in developing children's playgrounds to prevent juvenile delinquency.

The story goes that friends of Allen's were camping on Ausable Lake and were in an intense rainstorm in the Adirondacks. The storm was so catastrophic that it caused an avalanche. To mark this incident, one of Allen's comrades called a nameless peak "Allen" for Frederick Baylies Allen, who was not with them at the time. The name stood.

AMPERSAND MOUNTAIN

U.S.G.S. ELEVATION 3352 ft. (S.S.)

Northern Region, Franklin County, Town of Harrietstown

Verplanck Colvin credited Dr. William Watson Ely (1812-1879) with the Ampersand place name. Dr. Ely was known for his "Map of the New York Wilderness," which guided many people and put the Saranac Lakes: Lower, Middle, and Upper, on the map.

However, historians disagreed with where this mountain derived its name. Two theories predominate. Alfred L. Donaldson discussed one of these theories in his book, *A History of the Adirondacks*. He stated that Verplanck Colvin prefers the explanation he said in one of his reports,

"I attribute the name to the bright, yellow sandy shores and islands, which make it truly Amber-sand Lake."[4]

Stuart D. Ludlum, in his book, *Exploring the Adirondack Mountains 100 Years Ago*, stated a more common theory. He said, "It is such a crooked stream so bent and curved and twisted upon itself, so fond of turning around corners and sweeping away in great circles from its direct course, that its first explorers christened it after the eccentric supernumerary of the alphabet which appears in old spelling books as &."[5]

It is more likely that Verplanck Colvin was correct and that it came from amber sand because Ampersand Lake nearby had that color of sand. Undoubtedly, very few people in that era would have known about the symbol for the ampersand (&). The symbol is used in writing and printing to represent "and."

Ampersand was a vital mountain in Verplanck Colvin's Adirondack Survey because of the accurate readings that could be taken from, causing him to clear the tree-covered summit to make way for a survey station. Verplanck Colvin created the barren rock landscape for Ampersand Mountain, which today forms an opportunity for hikers to have a superb view of three Saranac Lakes: Upper, Middle, and Lower. Hikers can also see beyond these lakes on a clear day.

A fire tower on Ampersand Mountain was erected in 1911 and was disassembled in 1977 by New York State. Although the fire tower had many fire observers during its history, probably the most famous observer was Walter Channing Rice (1852-1924). He was an observer from 1915 to 1923 and earned the nickname "The Hermit of Amper-

---

4   Alfred L. Donaldson. *A History of the Adirondacks.* (New York: The Century Co., 1921), 1:38.

5   Stuart D Ludlum. *Exploring the Adirondack Mountains 100 Years Ago.* (Utica, NY: Brodock & Ludlum Publications 1972), 57.

sand" as he stayed up on the mountain from April until late fall. Far from a hermit, Rice was very much aware of what was going on in the world. Due to health issues, he was forced to leave his post in 1923 and passed away the following year. A tablet on a rock on Ampersand Mountain erected by his sons in 1930 commemorates this man's memory.

Ampersand, St. Regis, Baker, McKenzie, Scarface, and Haystack make up the Saranac Six Mountains. To become a Saranac Lake 6er, a hiker must climb the mountains as mentioned above. Upon completion, the hiker would go to Berkeley Green, located on Main and Broadway in downtown Saranac Lake. There the hiker would ring "The 6er Bell".

To acquire the Saranac Lake 6er patch and certificate with a number, the 6er hiker would pay ten dollars to the Village of Saranac Lake and complete all necessary information on the program entry. To become an "Ultra 6er," a hiker must leave Berkeley Green, climb all six mountains in a continuous 24-hour period, and ending at Berkeley Green.

ARAB MOUNTAIN
U.S.G.S. ELEVATION 2533 ft. (T.L.T.) F.T.
Northwestern Region, St. Lawrence County, Town of Piercefield

Arab is a corrupted word from an inaccurate translation of the French term, "arable," meaning "maple mountain." The French name for maple is erable, and the meaning of "erable" in French is an arid land.

Arab Mountain or Mount Arab, along with Coney and Goodman Mountains, make up the Tupper Lake Triad.

This hiking challenge began in 2015. Since everyone for various reasons cannot climb the forty-six highest peaks in the Adirondacks, there needed to be a challenge that individuals young and old, and families could attain to feel good about themselves and their accomplishments.

As a result, the Tupper Lake Triad was created by Charles Hoffer, director and a one-person band handling registration and website. People register, pay a fee and then start climbing the three mountains in as many days as they need to ascend them. The entire trail distance for the three mountains is 7.6 miles. Upon completing the three peaks, a person receives the Tupper Lake Triad patch, circular and depicts the three hikes. There is even a patch for a dog that completes the three walks.

Mount Arab houses a restored caretaker cabin with a small museum and a fire tower.

ARMSTRONG MOUNTAIN
U.S.G.S. ELEVATION 4360 ft. (H.H.)
High Peaks Region, Essex County, Town of Keene

Almon Thomas named this mountain for his friend and business associate, Thomas Armstrong. Thomas Armstrong, a well-known attorney and lumberman from Plattsburgh, New York, in Clinton County, and his business partner, Almon Thomas, purchased the Totten and Crossfield Purchase, consisting of about 28,000 acres of land and water. In 1887, the Adirondack Mountain Reserve purchased it and still owns part of it today.

AVALANCHE MOUNTAIN

U.S.G.S. ELEVATION 3809 ft. (H.H.)

High Peaks Region, Essex County, Town of Keene

Ancient landslides or avalanches occurring during pre-historic times on Avalanche gave the mountain its name. It was initially known as Caribou.

In 1868, Adirondack guide, Bill Nye, carried a lady named Matilda Fielding on his back across an underground ledge at Avalanche Lake adjacent to Avalanche Mountain. During the trip, Nye almost lost his balance while trying to keep her dry. Fielding's husband and her niece started laughing and yelled, "Hitch up, Matilda!" The expression stuck, and the place was forever famous in location and song. In the 1920s, logs were attached and bolted to Avalanche Mountain as a passageway across the lake. These catwalks were known as" Hitch-up Matildas."

AVERILL PEAK

U.S.G.S. ELEVATION 3806 ft. (H.H.)

Northern Region, Clinton County, Town of Saranac

Henry Ketcham (H.K.) Averill Jr. (1830-1918) was the son of a war hero in the Siege of Plattsburgh in 1814. This siege was under the command of General Alexander Macomb (Macomb Mountain). In honor of his gallantry, Henry's father, H.K. Averill, Sr. who was sixteen at the time of the battle, was honored by the United States Congress.

Henry Ketcham Averill Jr. became a well-known cartographer, author, photographer, and surveyor from Plattsburgh, New York. He surveyed the Northeastern Division of the Adirondack Survey, which covered all the land from Malone to Meacham Lake for Verplanck Colvin.

Averill's obituary in the Plattsburg Sentinel on April 2, 1918, best summarized his importance to Northern New York. It stated, "Mr. Averill will be well remembered by many of the townspeople here. A great many of the maps made in this section and the northern Adirondacks were the work of this surveyor and draftsman. His maps of Clinton county maps is still used extensively in this section."[6]

H.K. Averill died at the age of 88 at his daughter's house in East Hampton, Long Island, New York.

---

6 ___"Death of H.K. Averill." *Plattsburg Sentinel* (Plattsburg, NY). April 2, 1918.

B-ORONYMS

"Anyone who has stood upon a lofty summit and gazed over an inchoate tangle of deep canyons and cragged mountains, of sunlit lakelets and black expanses of forest, has become aware of a certain giddy sensation that there are no distances, no measures, simply unrelated matter rising and falling without any analogy to the banal geometry of breadth, thickness, and height."

—— BOB MARSHALL ——
Peak-Bagger, Author, and
Co-Founder of the Wilderness Society

B

BAKER MOUNTAIN

U.S.G.S. ELEVATION 2454 ft. (S.S.)

Northern Region, Essex County, Town of St. Armand

Baker Mountain, also referred to as Mount Baker, sits east of Saranac Lake Village with Moody Pond at its base. It was first climbed on March 11, 1916, by Edwin R. Stonaker on skis.

At one time, there was a nightclub known as the Mt. Baker Club at its base. The club featured women entertainers from Montreal and hid mobsters during Prohibition. Prohibition was a ban in the United States on everything that dealt with alcoholic beverages, including production, importation, transportation, and sales from 1920 to 1933.

One of the Saranac 6, Mount Baker, was named after Colonel Milote Baker and his son, Andrew, a pioneer family who lived in Saranac Lake. Milote Baker (1806-1870), with his wife, Susan, came from Keeseville, New York, to Saranac Lake in 1852 to raise his son Andrew Jackson and his three daughters, Narcissa, Emma, and Julia. He built a small store and one of the most famous Adirondack hotels for his livelihood. Colonel Baker later became Saranac Lake's first postmaster in 1854. After Colonel Baker died in 1874, the hotel and store ceased to exist.

As a young lad, Andrew (1840-1924) acted as a guide for the guests at his father's hotel and continued as a guide throughout his life, leading such famous people as New York Governor Horatio Seymour.

In 1866 Andrew built his family home on a knoll on a Saranac River bend. The Baker home was not far from his father's hotel on Pine Street.

In 1887 Andrew rented half of the house to well-known Scottish author Robert Louis Stevenson, who wrote *Treasure Island*. Stevenson had come to Saranac Lake because he had a lung condition thought to be tuberculosis and needed to be treated by the famous doctor, Dr. Edward Trudeau. While in the Baker house, Stevenson began writing *The Master of Ballantrae: A Winter's Tale* (published in 1889) about the two Scottish brothers (noblemen) who were at odds with one another during an uprising in their country. The Baker Family's home eventually became known to the world as the Robert Louis Stevenson Memorial Cottage.

BALD MOUNTAIN

U.S.G.S. ELEVATION 2313 ft. (RONDAXE 1912) F.T.

Southwestern Region, Herkimer County, Town of Webb

It was first called Pond Mountain by early settlers and trappers. Because of its rocky appearance, they soon began to refer to it as Bald.

In the 1870s, Verplanck Colvin used it as one of his survey points. In 1876 he said Bald should be renamed Mount St. Louis to honor early settlers who emigrated from St. Louis, Missouri, in the 1850s. Within a short time after

Colvin left the area, the name was changed back to Bald Mountain by the locals.

New York State constructed a fire tower on Bald Mountain in 1912. Since there was another Bald Mountain with a fire tower, Bald Mountain and its tower were renamed Rondaxe after a nearby lake. Rondaxe was a contraction of the word "Adirondack." Instead of spelling it "Rondacks," people spelled it as it sounded- "Rondaxe."

Today this mountain is a very popular climb for hikers, especially people with children, as it is easy and quick to reach the summit. From the top, climbers can see a great view of the Fulton Chain of Lakes. People continue to call it Bald Mountain.

BASIN MOUNTAIN

U.S.G.S. ELEVATION 4852 ft. (H.H.)

High Peaks Region, Essex County, Town of Keene

There isn't a definitive explanation for the name Basin Mountain. Some accounts stated that it was named by surveyor Verplanck Colvin and guide Ed Phelps. Historian Russell M. L. Carson believed that guide Old Mountain Phelps and artist Frederick S. Perkins called it Basin Mountain for the depression-like basin as they viewed it from another peak.

BIG SLIDE MOUNTAIN

U.S.G.S. ELEVATION 4232 ft. (H.H.)

High Peaks Region, Essex County, Town of Keene

In his book, *Peaks and People of the Adirondacks*, author, Russell Carson, wrote that "The name Big Slide (Mountain) came either from a great slide in 1830 on the Johns Brook side, or a later one on the South Meadow slope about 1856."[7] According to old mountain guides, Otis Estes, a resident of Keene Valley, named Big Slide in 1856.

BLAKE PEAK

U.S.G.S. ELEVATION 3976 ft. (H.H.)

High Peaks Region, Essex County, Town of Keene

Mills Blake (died 1930), Verplanck Colvin's best friend, became Verplanck Colvin's Chief Clerk and Assistant for the Adirondack Survey, putting him second in command of the Division of Levels. Russell Carson, author of *Peaks and People of the Adirondacks*, and Mills Blake's friends, including the Marshall brothers, named the mountain for Blake in 1924.

---

7   Russell M.L Carson. *Peaks and People of the Adirondacks.* (Glens Falls, NY: Adirondack Mountain Club 1973), 108.

BASIN MOUNTAIN, the ninth highest Adirondack mountain,
by Kay Flickinger *Courtesy of Adirondack Research Library*

BLUE MOUNTAIN
U.S.G.S. ELEVATION 3750 ft. (H.H.) F.T.
Central Region, Hamilton County, Town of Indian Lake

Blue Mountain had several previous names. The native people called it To-war-loon-da (Hill of Storms). The mountain for a brief time was called Mount Emmons for Ebeneezer Emmons, who was the New York State Geologist at that time and headed the first geological survey group of the Adirondacks.

However, Adirondack guides felt that Blue Mountain almost always appeared in shades of blue and was appropriately named. For a brief time, the mountain was called Mount Clinch in honor of Charles Powell Clinch (1797-1880), a member of the New York State Assembly and one of the Adirondack Survey promoters. Author Russell Carson said William Redfield, while traveling on the Steamboat "Franklin" on Lake Champlain in 1836, gave Blue Mountain its name not wanting to be confused with the Green Mountains of Vermont.

In 1876, Blue Mountain played an essential role during Verplanck Colvin's Survey. Colvin needed to have the surveying party members synchronize their watches with the Dudley Observatory in Albany, New York. So, at precisely 9:00 pm each night, he set off a series of powder flashes. These glitters of light would create such an event for the locals that they called it "Mr. Colvin's Fireworks."

The Blue Mountain House, a log hotel that stood on a mountain spur and built by an early resident, Miles Tyler Merlin, was named for the mountain. The hotel housed up to 100 guests. This hotel, later called the Merlin Hotel, was moved to the Adirondack Museum at Blue Mountain Lake (now the Adirondack Experience), where it sits on its grounds.

The National Register of Historic Places listed Blue Mountain's fire tower as worthy of preservation. One can observe many mountains from Blue Mountain's 360-degree view.

›→

BLUE RIDGE MOUNTAIN
U.S.G.S. ELEVATION 3451 ft. (H.H.)
Central Region, Essex County, Town of North Hudson

In 1872, Verplanck Colvin named a mountain that he observed from Little Moose Lake, Blue Ridge Mountain. His guides at the time renamed this mountain Colvin in honor of their leader at the time. Verplanck Colvin changed it to Cloud Cap ten years later. However, today this trailless peak continues as Blue Ridge Mountain.

BLUE RIDGE
U.S.G.S. ELEVATION 3697 ft. (H.H.)
Northern Region, Hamilton County, Town of Lake Pleasant

BLUE RIDGE RANGE
U.S.G.S. ELEVATION 3271 ft. (H.H.)
High Peaks Region, Essex County, Town of Schroon

BLUE RIDGE

U.S.G.S. ELEVATION 3189 ft. (H.H.)

Northern Region, Hamilton County, Town of Lake Pleasant

No one knows who named each of the above four Blue Ridge Mountains. According to the late Kelsie B. Harder, a professor and onomastician (one who studies etymology, history, and the use of proper names) at the State University of New York at Potsdam stated in his book, *Illustrated Dictionary of Place Names: United States and Canada*, a blue ridge is "descriptive of color, frequently in reference to haze on mountain peaks."[8]

BOREAS MOUNTAIN

U.S.G.S. ELEVATION 3779 ft. (H.H.)

High Peaks Region, Essex County, Town of North Hudson

Boreas is a synonym for north-wind, norther, and northerly. In Greek mythology, Boreas was the God of the North Wind and Winter. Also present in the area are Boreas River and Ponds.

In 1911 the state constructed a wooden fire tower on the mountain and replaced it with a steel one in 1919. It stood until 1988, when the state removed it.

---

8   Kelsie B. Harder, ed. *Illustrated Dictionary of Place Names: United States and Canada.* (New York: Van Nostrand Reinhold Company, 1976), 53.

BUELL MOUNTAIN

U.S.G.S. ELEVATION 3652 ft. (H.H.)

Central Region, Hamilton County, Town of Indian Lake

Buell Mountain could have derived its name from Buell Brook in Hamilton County, part of the Cedar River Flow, or one of the many Buel families inhabiting the county. The spelling is different, but the correct spelling often gets lost in translation as in other mountain entries.

Probably one of the most prominent of all the Buels was Sam Buel. Sam Buel lumbered a vast area of Hamilton County, owned a sawmill in the county, and served in the New York State Assembly.

BULLHEAD MOUNTAIN

U.S.G.S. ELEVATION 3314 ft.

Central Region, Warren County, Town of Johnsburg

According to Murray Heller in his book, *Call Me Adirondack*, water names such as Bullhead Pond were descriptive. They were generally straightforward in their meaning, so the pond must have been full of bullheads at one time. In this case, nearby Bullhead Mountain took the name after the nearby Bullhead Pond.

BURTONS PEAK
U.S.G.S. ELEVATION 3632 ft.
High Peaks Region, Essex County, Town of Keene

Hal Burton (1908-1992), a journalist, author, war hero, and Adirondack activist, once owned the Lost Brook Tract of land in Keene.

Born in Minneapolis, Minnesota, Hal Burton later studied journalism and became a writer for the *Saturday Evening Post, Life Magazine*, and the *New York Daily News*. He also published several books.

When World War II broke out, Burton became an officer in the renowned United States Army's Tenth Mountain Division. As an experienced alpine skier, Burton was called upon to train division troops in alpine skiing. He and other division members were involved in the Italian operation to take Mount Belvedere and Riva Ridge, which the Germans believed was impossible. The maneuver went down as one of the most daring raids in United States Military history.

After the war, he engaged again in journalism as an editorial writer for *Newsday*, a newspaper published on Long Island (New York). He wrote several books, including children's books about the Walton Boys and their outdoor adventures.

In 1971, Hal Burton published a book called *Ski Troops*. In his book, he described the history of early skiing in the United States. More importantly, he told how the amateur skiers formed United States Army's Tenth Mountain Division's ski troops during World War II and their heroic exploits. Following the war, these same ski veterans would establish American alpine resorts such as Vail, Aspen, and Whiteface.

Regarding skiing in the Adirondacks, Burton helped establish the Wright Peak Ski Trail and the Whiteface Mountain Ski Resort.

Pete Nelson, who later purchased Hal Burton's property, was able to have this mountain approved by the United States Board on Geographic Names. He had strong backing from local and state government agencies as well as Adirondack advocates. It was officially named Burtons Peak, not Burton's Peak, because no apostrophes or any punctuation are allowed in geographic names. Whatever the spelling, it does not detract from Hal Burton's importance in the United States, especially in the Adirondacks.

The first three forty-sixers Bob Marshall, Guide Herb Clark, and George Marshall

Courtesy of Adirondack Research Library

C-ORONYMS

"I searched the wilderness, ascended mountains, traced rivers to their sources, measured with mercurial barometer and hand level the heights of peaks and ridges, and unaware at that time, of the singular difficulties caused by magnetic iron and local attraction, endeavored to locate lakes and ponds from mountaintops, by compass bearings."

—— VERPLANCK COLVIN ——

Superintendent, The Adirondack Survey 1882

Adirondack Botanist and Naturalist Dr. Orra Phelps viewing
CASCADE MOUNTAIN, by Kay Flickinger
Courtesy of Adirondack Research Library

MOUNT COLDEN, the Birthplace of Adirondack Rock Climbing,
by Kay Flickinger *Courtesy of Adirondack Research Library*

CALAMITY MOUNTAIN
U.S.G.S. ELEVATION 3606 ft. (H.H.)

High Peaks Region, Essex County, Town of Newcomb

Calamity Mountain, Pond, and Brook were all named due to an incident that created quite the calamity which is written about in the Henderson Mountain entry.

CASCADE MOUNTAIN
U.S.G.S. ELEVATION 4094 ft. (H.H.)

High Peaks Region, Essex County, Town of Keene

Cascade Mountain, originally named Long Pond Mountain, and today one of the most famous climbs in the Adirondacks, was named for waterfalls that cascade down the mountain's side between two lakes at its base. Sidney and Warren Watson, who had built a nearby hotel near these falls around 1878, are responsible for naming the mountain, Cascade.

CELLAR MOUNTAIN

U.S.G.S. ELEVATION 3405 ft. (H.H.)

Northern Region, Hamilton County, Town of Arietta

This mountain was dubbed for nearby water bodies: Cellar Pond, Cellar Brook, and Cellar River. Root cellars were very popular and necessary in the eighteenth century to preserve and store vegetables and fruits for animal and human consumption. These cellars, usually built into the side of a hill or a stone structure, also held crops to sell at a market. When the refrigerator came into being, people no longer needed the root cellar.

CHENEY COBBLE

U.S.G.S. ELEVATION 3674 ft. (H.H.)

High Peaks Region, Essex County, Town of Newcomb

Born in New Hampshire, John Cheney (1800-1877) was one of the earliest and most legendary guides for Verplanck Colvin. He guided the scientific corps for Colvin, who made a geological survey of the Adirondack region. John Cheney always carried only a huge jackknife and a pistol when he guided. Two ponds also bear the renowned guide's name.

Cheney was made famous by Charles Fenno Hoffman, Ebenezer Emmons, Charles Lanman, William Redfield, and Farrand Benedict. Cheney said of himself, "Even from childhood, I was so in love with the woods that I not only neglected school, but was constantly borrowing a gun, or stealing the one belonging to my father…I was always the black sheep of the family."[9]

However, Cheney was far from the black sheep of the Adirondacks.

Many people didn't realize that Cheney was also a descriptive writer. He once said of the Adirondacks, as he viewed it from Mount Marcy,

"It makes a man feel what it is to have all creation placed beneath his feet. There are woods there which it would take a lifetime to hunt over; mountains that seem to shouldering each other, to boost the one whereon you stand up and away, heaven knows where. Thousands of little lakes are let in among them, so bright and clean that you would like to keep a canoe on each of them. Old Champlain, though 50 miles off, glistens below you like a strip of white birch bark, when slicked up by the moon on a frosty night; and the Green Mountains of Vermont beyond it fade and fade away, till they disappear as gradually as a cold scent when the dew rises."[10]

In 1877, after learning of John Cheney's death, Professor Farrand Benedict probably best summed up John Cheney: "I have always looked upon John (Cheney) as a necessary appendage to the Adirondacks, almost as necessary as Mt. Marcy itself. He has left a good name behind him--and this, (as the Biblical book of) Solomon says, is better than precious ointment."[11]

----

9   Charles Brumley. *Guides of the Adirondacks: A History: A Short Season-Hard Work-Low Pay.* (Utica, NY: North Country Books, Inc., 1994), 103.

10   Lincoln Barnett and the Editors of Time-Life Books. *The Ancient Adirondacks: The American Wilderness.* (New York: Time Inc., 1974), 77, 80.

11   Charles Brumley, *Guides of the Adirondacks,* 364.

CLIFF MOUNTAIN

U.S.G.S. ELEVATION 3940 ft. (H.H.)

High Peaks Region, Essex County, Town of Newcomb

Verplanck Colvin felt that there was only one name for this mountain Cliff for its series of cliffs.

MOUNT COLDEN

U.S.G.S. ELEVATION 4708 ft. (H.H.)

High Peaks Region, Essex County, Town of Keene

Robert Clarke and Alexander Ralph first ascended this peak in 1849 via the mountain's trap dike, which refers to steep bedding of large dark-colored igneous rocks. This mountain later became known as "Birthplace of Adirondack Rock Climbing."

The mountain first became known as Mount McMartin, named for Judge Duncan McMartin, one of the McIntyre Iron Works owners. In later writings, it was called both Mount McMartin and Mount Colden. Then Mc Martin was dropped, and it was called Mount Colden.

Colden was a New York socialite, an investor in the McIntyre Iron Works and a friend of David Henderson, the manager of the mine. Charles Dickens, another friend of David Colden, dedicated one of his books to his friend called *American Notes for General Circulation in 1842*, which detailed Charles Dickens' travels in America.

MOUNT COLVIN

U.S.G.S. ELEVATION 4049 ft. (H.H.)

High Peaks Region, Essex County, Town of Keene

"In Tribute to VERPLANCK COLVIN 1847-1920 Land Surveyor, Founder, and Champion of the New York State Forest Preserve and the Adirondack Park Remembered by his friends and admirers on the Centennial of the Adirondack Park-May 20, 1992."[12]

These are appropriate words placed on a plaque at his gravesite in Coeymans, New York and another one at the Beaver River Station on the Stillwater Reservoir. However, these words do not tell the whole story of Verplanck Colvin.

Verplanck Colvin (1847-1920), named for his mother's maiden name, Verplanck, was a native of Albany, New York. As a young man living in wealth and luxury, he was tutored at the family home on Western Avenue in Albany.

The homestead was called "The Elms" by local intellectuals. Colvin was an excellent writer and had a quest for science and mathematics. His family saw that he needed to further his education and accomplished this by sending him to The Albany Academy, followed by Nassau Academy, an excellent secondary institution. At Nassau Academy in Nassau, New York, Colvin met Mills Blake who became his lifelong best friend and right-hand man in the Adirondack Survey.

---

12 ___ "In Tribute to VERPLANCK COLVIN 1847-1920 Land Surveyor, Founder, and Champion of the New York State Forest Preserve and the Adirondack Park Remembered by his friends and admirers on the Centennial of the Adirondack Park-May 20, 1992." Accessed May 21, 2021. http://www.colvincrew.org/core/wp-content/uploads/RecoveryNo.-12.pdf.

Colvin wanted to attend the United States Military Academy at West Point, New York, but his father said no. Colvin had a love of the military and its strategies which were instrumental in conducting the Adirondack Survey.

Following his formal education, Verplanck and Mills worked in Colvin's father's law office for a short time. Verplanck felt he wanted more out of life and didn't want to work in law. Meeting author Alfred Street, and reading his book, *Woods and Waters: or, The Saranacs and Racket With Map of the Route and Nine Illustrations on Wood*, about Street's Adirondack adventures changed Colvin's life direction. As a result of this encounter, Verplanck became obsessed with doing more hiking and exploring, including the Adirondacks.

This desire eventually led him, in 1872, at a very young age, to the job of Superintendent of the Adirondack Survey. His right-hand man on this survey was his best friend, Mills Blake. Using funds Colvin acquired from the New York State Legislature and mostly his fortune, he spent 28 years of his life exploring and documenting the high peaks of the Adirondacks. He wrote reports for the legislature, as well as other personal writings and drawings regarding his findings. His work ended in 1900 when Governor of New York State, Theodore Roosevelt, turned Colvin's duties over to the New York State Engineer.

Colvin made many contributions to the field of Cartography. He aided cartographers by supplying them with basic information such as base, height, and distance to accurately calculate the proportions between contour lines and plot them on maps. His observations also helped geologists study the scratches and curves in the rocks leading to and from valleys, thereby helping them to interpret the direction of glacial movement through them.

His guides named the mountain Mount Colvin to honor their leader. Colvin was undoubtedly a Renaissance man, way ahead of his time with his ideas and what he accomplished in Adirondack Park. If not for his constant advocating, there would not be an Adirondack Park or Adirondack Forest Preserve today.

CONEY MOUNTAIN
U.S.G.S. ELEVATION 2264 ft. (T.L.T.)
Northwestern Region, St. Lawrence County, Town of Tupper Lake

In the century before Verplanck Colvin's survey, Coney Mountain was known as Peaked Mountain. Due to its proximity to the Franklin, St. Lawrence, and Hamilton counties' corner, Colvin later incorporated it in his triangulation network as Monument Mountain. On Stoddard's 1891 map, it appears as Cone Mountain, a corruption of Coney Mountain. It remains Coney Mountain today.

Its 360-degree rock face summit offers a marvelous view of the night sky and is of great interest to stargazers and astrophotographers.

COUCHSACHRAGA PEAK
U.S.G.S. ELEVATION 3793 ft. (H.H.)
High Peaks Region, Essex County, Town of Newcomb

Robert and George Marshall and their guide Herbert Clark first ascended this peak in 1924, and the Marshalls gave it its name for the Indian name for the Adirondack wilderness. Couchsachraga means "beaver hunting ground or habitation of winter" and "great and dismal wilderness." Most hikers equate with "dismal wilderness" for the nature of the climb.

D-ORONYMS

"If the fairest features of landscape are to be named after men, let them be the noblest and worthiest men alone..."

—— HENRY DAVID THOREAU ——

American Naturalist, Philosopher and Author

D

DIAL MOUNTAIN

U.S.G.S. ELEVATION 3980 ft. (H.H.)

High Peaks Region, Essex County, Town of Keene

This mountain, which has a northern and southern summit, has a name that is somewhat a mystery. Dial is the original name of the current Nippletop Mountain. The reason for the name switch to this mountain is unknown.

Keene Valley guides Ed Beebe and Ed Phelps (son of Old Mountain Phelps) first ascended Dial.

DIPPIKILL MOUNTAIN

U.S.G.S. ELEVATION 1562 ft.

Southeastern Region, Warren County, Town of Thurman

Dippikill Mountain, Pond, and trails are located on a 1000 plus acre plot of land owned and operated by the Student Association of the University at Albany (New York). The Faculty-Student Association of the New York State College for Teachers Albany Inc. purchased what is known today as Dippikill Wilderness Retreat for a ceremonial one dollar in 1956 from Irving P. Goodman.

Dutch settlers might have lived near Dippikill Pond and Mountain as Dippikill is a Dutch word meaning "small stream." The pond name occurred on earlier maps before the student association bought the property.

Dippikill Wilderness Retreat is the largest student-owned and operated wilderness retreat in the United States. Dippikill's mission is "to keep the area pristine, limit development, and offer visitors a glimpse of nature's beauty while enjoying overnight visits in rustic-style lodging."[13]

Open year-round, Dippikill has several lodges and campsites for students, staff, and alumni to rent and use. The retreat can accommodate up to 25 people.

Life is simple at Dippikill. Individuals who stay there must cut their wood to heat by and draw their water. It is a place where there is no television or cell service, just a place to get away from it all and enjoy nature. Henry David Thoreau would have loved Dippikill. This nineteenth-century author was best known for his book, *Walden*. In his book, Thoreau reflected on simple living in a natural world.

DIX MOUNTAIN

U.S.G.S. ELEVATION 4813 ft. (H.H.)

High Peaks Region, Essex County, Town of North Hudson

In 1837, Ebenezer Emmons named Dix Mountain for John Dix, Secretary of State for Governor William L. Marcy.

---

13 ___"Discover Dippikill." Accessed February 2, 2020. http://dippikill.com/about.

John Adams Dix (1798-1879) was born in Boscawen, New Hampshire, and joined the War of 1812 at the age of fourteen. After the war, he became a lawyer and journalist in Washington D.C. Dix married the daughter of a congressman and moved to Cooperstown in 1828. In 1833 he became the Secretary of State for New York, serving until 1838.

In addition to his position as Secretary of State, John Dix served New York State as governor, adjutant general, state superintendent of schools, United States Senator, and postmaster of New York City. He served as Secretary of Treasury for President Abraham Lincoln, a major general in the Union Army in America's Civil War, and U.S. minister to France. In his later years, he authored a series of travel essays on Europe that were very popular with Americans.

DONALDSON MOUNTAIN
U.S.G.S. ELEVATION 4062 ft. (H.H.)
High Peaks Region, Franklin County, Town of Harrietstown

Alfred Lee Donaldson (1866-1923) authored two volumes on Adirondack history. In 1895 after leaving a banking career in New York City due to poor health, Donaldson moved to Saranac Lake for its pure air and better climate. There he was treated for T.B. (Tuberculosis) by Dr. Edward Livingston Trudeau. Although his health never improved ultimately, he married, started banks and a telephone company in Saranac Lake, and served as village president and a trustee board member in the community.

To honor his friend Alfred Donaldson, historian Russell Carson, campaigned to have a mountain named after him, and Donaldson Mountain became official when accepted by the United States Board on Geographic Names in 1924.

DUN BROOK MOUNTAIN

U.S.G.S. ELEVATION 3563 ft. (H.H.)

Northern Region, Hamilton County, Town of Indian Lake

No one knows who coined the mountain's name. Dun means having a dull grayish brownish color. A brook nearby could have been such a grayish brownish color and been named Dun Brook. If that was the case, then the mountain nearby might have been named after that brook. Water bodies often received their names first in the Adirondacks.

E-ORONYMS

"The cluster of mountains in the neighborhood of the Upper Hudson and Ausable rivers, I propose to call the Adirondack Group, a name by which a well-known tribe of Indians who once hunted here may be commemorated."

—— **EBENEZER EMMONS** ——
Geologist, Report of the
Geological Survey of New York, 1838

E

MOUNT EMMONS
U.S.G.S. ELEVATION 4022 ft. (H.H.)

High Peaks Region, Franklin County, Town of Harrietstown

Born and raised in Middlefield, Massachusetts, in the Berkshire Mountains, Ebenezer Emmons (1799-1863) graduated from Williams College in Massachusetts with a degree in medicine in 1818. He had a brief career as a physician in Chester, Massachusetts.

After his medical career, he taught chemistry, mineralogy, and geology at his alma mater, Williams College. Longing for more schooling, Emmons attended the Rensselaer School, now Rensselaer Polytechnic Institute (R.P.I.) in Troy, New York, and graduated in the college's first class of 1826 in geology. A historical marker was placed on the R.P.I. campus highlighting his R.P.I. connection and his outstanding career. A further honor was bestowed on Emmons by his induction into the Rensselaer Alumni Hall Of Fame in 2007.

In 1828 he taught chemistry at Williams College, followed by a return to R.P.I. as a Junior Professor in Mineralogy and Geology.

He wrote several books on geology during his lifetime and was one of the prominent geologists.

In 1836, New York State Governor William Learned Marcy appointed Ebenezer Emmons to be the State Geologist for the Northern New York State Geological District to conduct the geological survey of Northern New York State (Counties of Essex, Clinton, Hamilton, Warren, Saint Lawrence, Franklin, and Jefferson), including the Adirondacks. In 1837, Emmons, with other scientists, would organize and lead the first ascent of Mount Marcy, and they named it for Governor Marcy. The following year, Emmons called the mountain ranges in New York State the "Adirondack" and the "Taconic" Mountains. Emmons completed his survey in 1842.

In 1852 Emmons was appointed state geologist for the state of North Carolina.

Following his death in Brunswick, North Carolina, his body was moved and was buried at the Albany Rural Cemetery in New York.

⇥

ESTHER MOUNTAIN

U.S.G.S. ELEVATION 4232 ft. (H.H.)

High Peaks Region, Essex County, Town of Wilmington

Esther, one of the 46 highest mountains, was the first mountain named for a woman, and there would not be another one until 2015 when Grace Peak replaced East Dix.

Esther McComb, an adventurous fifteen-year-old girl, set out to climb what would later be known as Whiteface Mountain in the early nineteenth century, despite her parents' wishes. It turned out that she was not on Whiteface Mountain but a neighboring nameless mountain. While exploring the mountain, Esther became lost. Searchers found her the next day. After the incident, her mother jokingly called the mountain Esther. The name stuck, according to historian Russell Carson.

Grace Hudowalski, who also climbed her first mountain, Mount Marcy, described what it must have been like for Esther McComb to climb the peak at fifteen. Grace said, "She pushed on through brush and tall trees, scaled bump after bump, and pulled herself over ledges until she finally stood atop her mountain…she had climbed a mountain for pleasure. Unheard of! For Adventure. Incredible!"[14]

In 1923, Wallace Goodspeed, whose family was one of the first settlers near today's Esther Mountain, told the story he had heard as a boy to Charles Beede, a famous Keene Valley guide. Beede retold the story to the author, Russell Carson. Carson later published it in his book, *Peaks and People of the Adirondacks*.

Locals called the mountain, Esther. Outsiders did not even know it existed until C.H. Burt mentioned it his book, *The Opening of the Adirondacks* in 1865. Even Ebenezer Emmons did not see this 4200+foot mountain behind Whiteface Mountain when he surveyed the area.

Both Whiteface and Esther share the same ridge, so what history Whiteface has had is also Esther's. They share the Whiteface Memorial Highway, the Olympic 1932 cross country trail, the ski center, and America's first family theme park, Santa's Workshop, North Pole, New York.

14   Grace Hudowalski. "Esther." *The Cloudsplitter* (April 1939), 4.

F-ORONYMS

"Mountains are more satisfying because they are more individual. It is possible to feel a very strong attachment for a certain range whose outline has grown familiar to our eyes, or a clear peak that has looked down, day after day, upon our joys and sorrows, moderating our passions with its calm aspect."

—— HENRY VAN DYKE ——

American Educator, Diplomat,
Clergyman and Author of *Little Rivers*

F

FISHING BROOK MOUNTAIN
U.S.G.S. ELEVATION 3550 ft. (H.H.)
Northern Region, Essex County, Town of Minerva

The highest of the two Fishing Brook Mountains is mentioned several times in the New York State Department of Environmental Conservation in their writings. This department does not explain Fishing Brook Mountain's name origin.

A brook called Fishing Brook lies on the slope of this mountain. Like Brown Pond Mountain previously mentioned in this book, one might assume that Fishing Brook Mountain derives its name from the brook found on this mountain. Also, Henry Abbott, in his book, *Fishing Brook*, refers to this brook as appropriately named with its abundance of trout.

The epicenter of a 5.2 magnitude earthquake on October 7, 1983, was located near this mountain.

FISHING BROOK RANGE
U.S.G.S. ELEVATION 3268 ft. (HH-91)
Northern Region, Essex County, Town of Minerva

This peak marks the end of a long ridge. It leads southwest from Fishing Brook Mountain and is the smaller of the two.

G-ORONYMS

"A man does not climb a mountain without bringing some of it away with him and leaving something of himself upon it."

—— **SIR MARTIN CONWAY** ——

British Mountaineer and Cartographer

G

GIANT MOUNTAIN
U.S.G.S. ELEVATION 4623 ft. (H.H.)
High Peaks Region, Essex County, Town of Keene

As its name implies, Giant is a massive mountain that rises above all other peaks in its area. It blocks the High Peaks' views to the west and provides the High Peaks' best view to the east.

It is questionable as to who was the first person to climb Giant Mountain. Historian Russell Carson stated that the surveyor, Charles Broadhead, and his crew that first ascended it.

Old Mountain Phelps contends it was the famous geologist Arnold Guyot who climbed it in 1863. Guyot saw a giant slide that resembled the figure of a giant. Guyot may have given Giant its name.

Early residents of Pleasant Valley, now present-day Elizabethtown, called the mountain "Giant of the Valley."

GOODMAN MOUNTAIN
U.S.G.S. ELEVATION 2162 ft. (T.L.T.)
Northwestern Region, Franklin County, Town of Tupper Lake

This mountain, formerly named Litchfield, was owned by a wealthy local landowner nearby. In 2002, Litchfield was renamed Goodman Mountain for Andrew Goodman (1943-1964), whose family spent summer vacations in the Tupper Lake area. Several times as a kid, Andrew, who climbed this mountain, played a role in the United States Civil Rights movement.

Few people realize vital connections between the Adirondack Mountains and the many events in American history. Andrew Goodman was one of those connections.

Andrew Goodman, who as a child summered near Tupper Lake, wanted to make a difference by helping others. In 1964 at the young age of 20, this college student traveled to Mississippi and worked with another New Yorker, Michael Schwerner, and Mississippian resident James Chaney during Freedom Summer to aid in voter registration of African-Americans. After the notification of a local sheriff of these young men's actions, the Ku Klux Clan kidnapped and killed the three civil rights workers. In 1988, a movie entitled *Mississippi Burning*, starring Gene Hackman and William Dafoe, depicted this event.

In 2014, President Barak Obama awarded the three men the Presidential Medal of Freedom. In a news release, the Democratic Senator from New York State, Kirsten Gillibrand, who sponsored this legislation for the medal, said, "James Chaney, Andrew Goodman, and Michael Schwerner were unsung heroes who sacrificed their lives in the fight for freedom, justice, and equality for all."[15] Senator Gillibrand also said she would work for these three to receive the Congressional Gold Medal. She remarked, "Voting is one of the most sacred rights we have as Amer-

---

15   Kim Smith Dedam. "Andrew Goodman to receive posthumous Medal of Freedom." *Press-Republican* (Plattsburgh, NY), November 12, 2014.

icans, and it is important for us to reflect on our past and honor those who have fought to ensure every citizen has access to that basic freedom."[16]

GORE MOUNTAIN

U.S.G.S. ELEVATION 3199 ft. (H.H.) F.T.

Central Region, Warren County, Town of Johnsburg

Gore Mountain is best known today as one of three ski areas owned and operated by New York State. The other two mountains are Whiteface Mountain in the Adirondacks and Belleayre Mountain in the Catskill Mountains.

In the early days of the Adirondacks, farmers and loggers found Gore Mountain too steep and worthless. A gore, by definition, was an unsurveyed tract of land. Gore Mountain remained unsurveyed during the early days, and farmers and loggers called it a "gore." The name stuck as Gore Mountain.

During the first half of the twentieth century, Gore Mountain supplied 90% of the world's garnets' supply. Garnets were helpful in the production of abrasives. Nearby Garnet Hill, a cross country ski area, derives its name from these garnets.

In 1933, Brothers Carl and Vincent Schaefer developed skiing on the mountain.

The Gore Ski Area had many firsts: a ski patrol, rope tows, recorded ski race, the T-bar lift, and snow train carrying members of the Winter Sports Club from Schenectady, New

---

16   Dedam, "Andrew Goodman."

York to the ski area. A trail at Gore Mountain commemorates the Schaefer Brothers: Carl, Vincent, and Paul, who was a well-known Adirondack conservationist and writer.

$$\rightarrow$$

GOTHICS

U.S.G.S. ELEVATION 4724 ft. (H.H.)

High Peaks Region, Essex County, Town of Keene

Old Man Mountain Phelps and his artist friend, Frederick Perkins, observed rock slides on a mountain near Mount Marcy that resembled Gothic architecture and coined Gothics' name.

James Storrow and Orlando Beede first climbed the mountain.

$$\rightarrow$$

GRACE PEAK

U.S.G.S. ELEVATION 4006 ft. (H.H.)

High Peaks Region, Essex County, Town of North Hudson

On June 12, 2014, Grace Peak (mountain), originally known as East Dix Mountain, was named officially by the United States Board on Geographic Names for Grace Leach Hudowalski (1906-2004), the first woman and the ninth person to climb all forty-six highest New York State peaks.

Doug Arnold chaired a committee to change the name of East Dix to Grace Peak. This process was lengthy but ultimately led to its renaming.

East Dix Mountain renamed to GRACE PEAK in 2014
after Grace Hudowalski, by Kay Flickinger
Courtesy of Adirondack Research Library

In the Fall 2014 edition of *Adirondack Peeks,* a magazine of the Adirondack Forty-Sixers, Doug Arnold remarked, "In today's world, reality- T.V. stars, overpaid sports figures, and egocentric politicians are offered up to us by the media as our heroes. With the naming of Grace Peak, it is refreshing to know that a woman, born in 1906, who made such a positive impact on so many lives and whose love of the Adirondacks has had so many far-reaching effects is now recognized for her lifelong passion."[17]

Grace was the president and the historian for the well-known Forty Sixers Organization. A person becomes a forty-sixer by climbing the forty-six highest New York State peaks (all located in the Adirondacks) and docu-

---

17   Doug Arnold. "Grace Peak: A Personal Reflection."
      Adirondack Peeks 51, no. 2 (Fall 2014): 5.

menting his/her climbs. During her fifty-nine years as a historian, Grace wrote more than sixty thousand letters to aspiring hikers about wanting to climb all the forty-six peaks. Grace often told hikers the advice given to her by her father on her first climb of Mount Marcy, "It's not important whether you make it to the summit... what's important is how you make the climb."[18]

To learn more about Grace's accounts of her climbs and her love for the mountains and its people, watch the documentary, *The Mountains Will Wait for You*, directed by Fredrick Schwoebel and narrated by singer-songwriter Johnny Cash.

Grace passed away in Guilderland Center, New York, shortly after the film's release at ninety-eight. Her legacy will live on through her named mountain and many letters sent to hikers throughout the years.

GRAY PEAK

U.S.G.S. ELEVATION 4800 ft. (H.H.)

High Peaks Region, Essex County, Town of Keene

Professor Asa Gray (1810-1888), a famous nineteenth-century Harvard botanist, worked in the southern Adirondacks far from his namesake, Gray Peak. Russell Carson believes this oronym was coined by Professor J. A. Lintner, the New York State Entomologist, around 1869.

The first recorded ascent of this mountain was by Verplanck Colvin and Guide William B. Nye (Bill) in 1872.

---

18   Arnold, "Grace Peak", 5.

GREEN MOUNTAIN

U.S.G.S. ELEVATION 3976 ft. (H.H.)

High Peaks Region, Essex County, Town of Keene

On an earlier map, Green had a third "e," Greene. On later maps, Green Mountain lost its final "e."

No one knows who dubbed it Green and or its name origin. Early residents could have given it the name since the mountain had an abundance of coniferous trees.

In the summer of 1893, G. Locke and his Colvin Adirondack Survey party ascended Green Mountain.

H-ORONYMS

"What would be ugly in a garden constitutes beauty in a mountain."

—— VICTOR HUGO ——

French Author

HADLEY MOUNTAIN

U.S.G.S. ELEVATION 2651 ft.

Southeastern Region, Saratoga County, Town of Hadley

Hadley, New York was probably named for Hadley, Massachusetts, by the Jeffers' Family. The Jeffers' Family emigrated from Hadleigh, Wales and settled in western Massachusetts. Eventually, they relocated to what today is known as Hadley, New York. Hadley Mountain derives its place name from the nearby village of Hadley.

MOUNT HAYSTACK

U.S.G.S. ELEVATION 4924 ft. (H.H.)

High Peaks Region, Essex County, Town of Keene

This mountain's summit resembled a pile of rocks in the form of a haystack, prompting Orson Scofield (Old Mountain) Phelps to dub it Haystack. Phelps, Almeron Oliver, and George Estey first ascended it.

Verplanck Colvin called Mount Haystack "The Matterhorn of the Adirondacks," considered the High Peaks' best view. Matterhorn is a high mountain in Switzerland that many climbers have ascended.

Mount Haystack ranks first with those who have climbed it because of its magnificent view of the other peaks.

⇒

HAYSTACK MOUNTAIN
U.S.G.S. ELEVATION 2871 ft. (S.S.)
High Peaks Region, Essex County, Town of North Elba

Like the higher peak bearing the same name, Haystack Mountain is haystack-shaped.

⇒

HENDERSON MOUNTAIN
U.S.G.S. ELEVATION 3707 ft. (H.H.)
High Peaks Region, Essex County, Town of Newcomb

David Henderson (1807-1845) was an administrator at the McIntyre Iron Works and son-in-law of its owner, Archibald McIntyre.

On September 3, 1845, David Henderson, his son, Archie, and Guide John Cheney were scouting the Iron Works area to find the best place to divert the Hudson and Opalescent Rivers' waters. They needed this to provide water power for the bellows of the Iron Works' blast furnaces. While searching, they came upon a small pond with ducks on it. Henderson gave Cheney a pistol to shoot the birds. Cheney failed to fire the gun before the ducks flew away. Cheney handed back the weapon to Henderson, who placed the weapon in his knapsack on a rock. The gun discharged and fatally wounded Henderson.

David Henderson was quite the entrepreneur and a visionary. Had he lived, the Adirondacks might look quite different today with a vast iron ore industry.

In 1850 to commemorate their father's life, the children had a monument constructed near the site where he lost his life. The memorial is still visible today.

HOFFMAN MOUNTAIN

U.S.G.S. ELEVATION 3701 ft. (H.H.)

High Peaks Region, Essex County, Town of Schroon

Anthony Hoffman surveyed the current land of the Minerva and Schroon townships near his namesake.

Mr. Hoffman was a local politician from Dutchess County who served in the New York State government and on the New York State Board of Regents.

Hoffman Mountain was also called Schroon Mountain because of its proximity to Schroon Lake. In 1838, one of the most well-known Hudson River School of artists, Thomas Cole, painted a picture of Hoffman Mountain. This painting was named one of Cole's best wilderness paintings. Cole remarked, "This peak created a feeling of vastness and awe which the artist translated into a scene of mystery and danger obscurity and solitude."[19]

---

19   Barbara McMartin and Lee Brenning. *Discover the West Central Mountains: A Guide to the Western Wildernesses and the Moose River Plains.* (Woodstock, VT: Backcountry Publications, 1988), 24.

HOUGH PEAK
U.S.G.S. ELEVATION 4393 ft. (H.H.)
High Peaks Region, Essex County, Town of North Hudson

Known initially as Middle Dix, Little Dix, and Marshall Mountains, the New York State Committee on Geographic Names, in 1937, settled on the name Hough to honor Dr. Benjamin Franklin Hough.

Benjamin Franklin Hough (1822-1885) grew up on the western side of the Adirondacks in Martinsburg, New York, near Lowville. As a boy, he had an interest in mineralogy and hiking long distances. His father died when Benjamin was only eight years old. From that point on, Benjamin went by his middle name, Franklin.

In 1843 Franklin graduated from Union College in Schenectady, New York, and continued his education at Western Reserve College in Cleveland, Ohio, where he received a medical degree in 1848.

Practicing medicine only briefly, he left the medical field to research. He published several books on the history of various New York State counties, including Jefferson, Lewis, St. Lawrence, and Franklin.

While working as United States Superintendent of the Census, he discovered the New York State's declining forests. The discovery of forest destruction led him to the conservation of forests. Later he was appointed as the head of what is now called the United States Forestry Agency. Because of his work in the forestry field, he received the nickname "Father of American Forestry."

He died at his home in Lowville, New York.

HURRICANE MOUNTAIN

U.S.G.S. ELEVATION 3688 ft. (H.H.) F.T.

High Peaks Region, Essex County, Town of Elizabethtown

No-de-ne-yo is the Indian name for Hurricane Mountain. The meaning of this Indian name is "Hill of Wind," and as strong winds often hit it, what better name than Hurricane for this mountain.

In the 2019 edition of *Outside Magazine*, Hurricane Mountain was named the best hike in New York State.

I-ORONYMS

"*Great things are done when men and mountains meet.*
This is not done by jostling in the street."

—— **WILLIAM BLAKE** ——

English Poet, Painter and Printmaker

I

MOUNT INEZ

U.S.G.S. ELEVATION 1552 ft.

High Peaks Region, Essex County, Town of Lewis

Mount Inez is named for Inez Milholland (Boissevain). She was a leader of the women's suffrage movement and the fourth woman in the Adirondack Park to have a mountain named in her honor. The other three mountains are Mount Esther, Mount Jo, and Grace Peak.

Inez Milholland (1886-1916) was born into a wealthy family in Brooklyn, New York but spent her summers on her family land, Meadowmount, in Lewis, Essex County. She graduated from Vassar College in Poughkeepsie, New York, and received a law degree from New York University School of Law.

Aside from being a lawyer, Inez is best known for her civil causes. She promoted world peace, prison reform, African Americans' rights, and a woman's right to vote. She was famous for leading a women's suffrage parade, wearing a white cape and a crown on a large white horse on the eve of President Woodrow Wilson's inauguration in Washington, D.C., on March 3, 1913 and became known as the "Suffrage Joan of Arc."

In 1916, she toured the western United States, speaking on behalf of women's rights, despite being plagued by an illness known as pernicious anemia or deficiency of B-12, causing not enough red blood cells to be produced. During a speech on women's rights in Los Angeles, California, she died at age thirty, before the passage of the nineteenth amendment in 1920, giving women the right to vote. Her body was taken to her summer home in Lewis, New York where she was laid to rest.

After her death, her father, John Milholland (the pneumatic tube's inventor), persuaded the Lewis townspeople to rename Mount Discovery for his daughter. However, it was not until December 12, 2019, that Mount Discovery was officially renamed Mount Inez by the United States Board on Geographic Names.

IROQUOIS PEAK

U.S.G.S. ELEVATION 4829 ft. (H.H.)

High Peaks Region, Essex County, Town of Newcomb

Verplanck Colvin first called this mountain, Mount Clinton, to honor Governor Dewitt Clinton, but about 1880, he changed it to Iroquois. He always favored the memory of the Native American, so he named the second-highest mountain in the MacIntyre Range, Mount Iroquois, after the Native American people whose hunting territory was in the Adirondacks. Today it is called Iroquois Peak.

J-ORONYMS

*"To go places and do things that have never been
done before – that's what living is all about."*

—— MICHAEL COLLINS ——

Apollo 11 Command Module Pilot Astronaut

J

JAY MOUNTAIN

U.S.G.S. ELEVATION 3379 ft. (H.H.)

High Peaks Region, Essex County, Town of Lewis

Often, a mountain is dubbed after the town it is located in, as in the case of the Town of Jay, 68.3 square miles nearby in Northeastern Essex County. John Jay (1745-1829), Governor of New York State (1795-1801), also served at the federal government level as a Provincial Congress member and chief justice of the United States Supreme Court (1789-1795) under President George Washington.

MOUNT JO

U.S.G.S. ELEVATION 2813 ft.

High Peaks Region, Essex County, Town of North Elba

Henry Van Hoevenberg named Mount Jo for his fiancée, Josephine (Jo) Schofield in 1877. She passed away before they could marry. You can read more of Josephine's story in the Mount Van Hoevenberg oronym later in this book.

K-ORONYMS

"It isn't important if you reach the summit… what matters is how you make the climb. We were never lost, but there were lots of times when we didn't know where we were."

—— GRACE HUDOWALSKI ——

The first woman to become an Adirondack 46'er.

KILBURN MOUNTAIN

U.S.G.S. ELEVATION 3868 ft. (H.H.)

High Peaks Region, Essex County, Town of Wilmington

Kilburn Mountain and Kilburn Slide are prominent geographic features in the Adirondacks. One can learn about area landmark names by speaking to locals and historical societies. A Stephenson clan member, whose family name is associated with the Stephenson Range, shed some light on this mountain.

Wilmington's Kilburn family-owned and logged the land across the road from what today is Route 86. Ransom Kilburn was involved with this property and later sold it to the State of New York.

It was not uncommon to have geographic features named after families who owned the land or lived nearby.

L-ORONYMS

"You can never conquer the mountain.
You can only conquer yourself."

—— JAMES WHITTAKER ——

American Mountaineer and Guide

L

LEWEY MOUNTAIN

U.S.G.S. ELEVATION 3665 ft. (H.H.)

Central Region, Hamilton County, Town of Lake Pleasant

Contrary to many tourist websites, Lewey Lake and nearby Lewey Mountain did not receive their namesakes from the famous Hermit French Louie. Lewey Lake and Mountain received their names before French Louie appeared on the scene. According to Ted Aber and Stella King in their book, *The History of Hamilton County*, Lewey Lake received its name from Lewis Elijah Sabael (1797-1860), who lived in the area. Many times, a nearby mountain will take on the name of the adjacent water body.

Native American Trapper Lewis Elijah Sabael guided David Henderson, who was in the region looking for silver and iron ore deposits in 1826. Sabael was paid $1.50 and given a plug of tobacco for his efforts. Many people felt for years that Sabael was paid too much for this endeavor. Henderson's father-in-law, Archibald McIntyre, whom the McIntyre Range was named, later established his Iron Works on this spot.

LITTLE MOOSE MOUNTAIN
U.S.G.S. ELEVATION 3609 ft. (H.H.)
Central Region, Hamilton County, Town of Arietta

Moose, one of the most iconic creatures, roamed the Adirondack Park in the early days. Many place names in New York State took their names from this animal. Today, the moose is making a comeback after almost being exterminated in the 1800s due to deforestation overhunting.

※——➤

LITTLE SANTANONI MOUNTAIN
U.S.G.S. ELEVATION 3471 ft. (H.H.)
High Peaks Region, Essex County, Town of Newcomb (See Santanoni)

※——➤

LOWER WOLFJAW MOUNTAIN
U.S.G.S. ELEVATION 4190 ft. (H.H.)
High Peaks Region, Essex County, Town of Keene

The Indian Pass, a book by Alfred Street, stated that the painter, Arthur Wyand, was credited with painting and naming the two summits of Upper and Lower Wolfjaws. He chose this name as when you see the mountains together, they resembled a wolf's jaws.

LYON MOUNTAIN

U.S.G.S. ELEVATION 3829 ft. (H.H.) F.T.

Northern Region, Clinton County, Town of Saranac

In one of his reports, Surveyor Verplanck Colvin stated that the highest point in Clinton County was for Saranac settler Nathaniel Lyon.

Nathaniel Lyon, born in Vermont, became an early settler in the Saranac River Valley around 1803 and settled near the highest mountain in the area, later his namesake. During the War of 1812, fearing bands of Indians would attack the Saranac River Valley, Nathaniel Lyon left the valley and returned to his native Vermont until the war was over. He then returned to the Saranac Valley to farm for the rest of his life. Nathaniel's granddaughter, Hattie Lyon, became the first female to climb the mountain named for him.

Nathaniel Lyon (1818-1861), a relative of this Saranac Valley resident, was a highly decorated United States Army general and the Commander of Union Forces in Missouri during America's Civil War. He was killed in a battle at Wilson's Creek, Missouri, but by his heroic actions, Missouri did not become a Confederate state.

M-ORONYMS

ARTICLE 14 OF THE NEW YORK STATE CONSTITUTION (November 1894)

It states, *"The lands of the state, now owned or hereafter acquired, constituting the forest preserve as now fixed by law, shall be forever kept as wild forest lands. They shall not be leased, sold, or exchanged, or be taken by any corporation, public or private, nor shall the timber thereon be sold, removed, or destroyed"*. This article is known as the "Forever Wild Clause."

M

MACNAUGTON MOUNTAIN
U.S.G.S. ELEVATION 3983 ft. (H.H.)
High Peaks Region, Essex County, Town of North Elba

Some of the early books on this region called this toponym Henderson Mountain for David Henderson, the McIntyre Iron Works, and the son-in-law of its owner, Archibald McIntyre. For some unknown reason, a mountain nearby was renamed Henderson.

MacNaughton Mountain, named for James MacNaughton (1851-1905), a grandson of McIntyre, was trailless. James MacNaughton accompanied Theodore Roosevelt on his famous climb of Mount Marcy on September 13, 1901.

MACOMB MOUNTAIN
U.S.G.S. ELEVATION 4396 ft. (H.H.)
High Peaks Region, Essex County, Town of North Hudson

Alexander Macomb (1782-1841) was born in British-held Detroit to a wealthy merchant and fur trader. After the Revolutionary War, he and his family moved to New York City. He received his early education in Newark, New Jersey, and graduated from the United States Military Academy at West Point.

During the American War of 1812 Alexander Macomb, became a hero in the Land Battle of Plattsburg in 1814. With a force of fifteen hundred troops, he defeated over ten thousand British troops.

Later in his career, he was appointed Commander-in-Chief of the United States Army and is known for writing the first court-martial regulations, creating army pensions, and advocating for death benefits for spouses.

》—→

MOUNT MARCY
U.S.G.S. ELEVATION 5344 ft. (H.H.)
High Peaks Region, Essex County, Town of Keene

In 1837, Ebenezer Emmons, a chemistry professor at Williams College in Massachusetts, and David Henderson, William Redfield, Archibald McIntyre, and others set out on a geological expedition to explore the Adirondack Mountains. They were hoping to find the source of the Hudson River.

On August 5, 1837, this expedition climbed what is now known as the highest peak in New York. Ebenezer Emmons and others in the group decided to name the mountain Mount Marcy after the then-seated governor, William Learned Marcy. Emmons would later be criticized for the name choice as citizens did not want it named after a politician. Many people liked the name, Tahawus, meaning "cloud-splitter," which many thought to be an early Native American name, but Tahawus was the invention of Charles Hoffman, an early newspaperman.

William Learned Marcy (1786-1857) served New York well. Before being the governor, Marcy long served the

A snowy view of MOUNT MARCY, Kay Flickinger

Courtesy of Adirondack Research Library

state as a teacher, lawyer, soldier in the War of 1812, the State Comptroller, associate justice of the New York State Supreme Court, and a United States Senator. Following his service as a four-year term as Governor of New York State, Marcy would go on to serve his country again at the federal level. He served as Secretary of State for President Franklin Pierce and Secretary of War for President James Polk.

Marcy never wanted to climb his namesake. He might have traveled through the area when he was serving in the army during 1812.

William Learned Marcy also had a village and a state hospital in New York State named after him.

Mount Marcy has a more recent distinction. In January of 2004, N.A.S.A. (the National Aeronautics and Space Administration) landed the robotic rover, Spirit, on the planet of Mars. Spirit relayed this planet's images back to scientists at the Jet Propulsion Laboratory in Pasadena, California on earth. The scientists from the laboratory gave rocks found on Mars names. One such rock looked like

In 2004 on Mars the Spirt rover approached a football-sized rock which scientists dubbed - Adirondack *Courtesy of NASA JPL*

the pyramid-shaped mountain, Mount Marcy, the highest peak in the Adirondack Range. So, the scientist who had climbed Mount Marcy named the rock "Adirondack."

MOUNT MARSHALL
U.S.G.S. ELEVATION 4380 ft. (H.H.)
High Peaks Region, Essex County, Town of Newcomb

Mount Marshall, formerly called Mount (Dewitt) Clinton, was named for Robert (Bob) Marshall, son of Louis Marshall, a New York City corporate, civil rights, constitutional lawyer, and an avid conservationist. The Marshalls and five other families bought a large property on Lower Saranac Lake, where Louis Marshall built an Adirondack Great Camp called "Knollwood."

Louis Marshall and others framed Article 14 of the New York State Constitution, which created the "Forever Wild Clause" to establish the New York State Forest Preserve.

Also, Louis Marshall created the State University College of New York Environmental Science and Forestry Program (SUNY ESF) at Syracuse University.

Robert Marshall (1901-1939) was a highly educated individual, receiving degrees from SUNY ESF, Harvard University, and a Ph.D. from John Hopkins University in Plant Physiology.

Robert Marshall loved the outdoors and spent time in the Adirondacks with his brother, George, and a family friend and guide, Herb Clark. From 1918 to the 1920s, the trio was the first to climb all the 46 peaks thought to be over 4000 feet.

Bob Marshall worked for the Bureau of Indian Affairs and the United States Forest Service. While working for the Forest Service, he spent much time in Montana and the Arctic Wildernesses. The "Bob Marshall Wilderness" in Western Montana was a legacy for Robert Marshall, a conservationist, author, co-founder of the Wilderness Society, and many other achievements.

After Bob Marshall's death, the Adirondack Forty-Sixers petitioned the New York State Committee on Geographic Names to change the name Mount Clinton to Mount Marshall.

MCKENZIE MOUNTAIN
U.S.G.S. ELEVATION 3842 ft. (H.H., S.S.)
Northern Region, Essex County, Town of North Elba

Verplanck Colvin climbed the mountain in 1878 and was known to name a mountain after descending it. He likely named it after one of his favorite guides, Rod McKenzie, who had recently passed away. Rod McKenzie from Keene Valley climbed Gothics with Colvin and Old Mountain Phelps in August 1873.

More recently, one of the prominent men from Saranac Lake, Thomas B. Cantwell, was very taken in by McKenzie Mountain. Thomas Cantwell, a graduate of Williams College in Massachusetts and Albany Law School, was a huge community servant for Saranac Lake and its surrounding area. As a local attorney and civil servant he served his community in many ways, including being a member of the Masonic Lodge and Rotary Clubs, being an active supporter of the Boy Scouts, building the first ski tow on Mount Pisgah, rejuvenating the Saranac Winter Carnival which is known near and far and serving the Trudeau Institute and the North Country Community College. It was because of all that he did for his community that "The Community Room" at the Saranac Lake Free Library was named for him.

Mr. Cantwell was interested in establishing a ski resort on McKenzie Mountain because of its large snowfall amounts starting in autumn and retention of the snow into May. He could frequently be found taking the measure of snow depths on McKenzie Mountain in the 1950s. He also took many aerial photographs and mapped out plans for trails and chairlifts. He formed a ten-man joint Saranac Lake-Lake Placid committee who shared in his vision of a ski resort on McKenzie Mountain, but Whiteface Mountain was developed in 1958 instead. Following Mr. Cantwell's passing in 1977, his ashes were scattered across McKenzie Mountain.

Because of his father's involvement in McKenzie Mountain, his son T. Barry and wife, Peg Cantwell, named their first child McKenzie who was born nine months after the father's passing. Since then, Thomas Cantwell's granddaughter, McKenzie (Cantwell) Jones, has climbed the mountain and has become a prominent Nurse Practitioner in New York's Capital Region. She is serving people just like her grandfather except in a different manner.

MOOSE MOUNTAIN

U.S.G.S. ELEVATION 3868 ft. (H.H., S.S.)

High Peaks Region, Essex County, Town of St. Armand

Moose Mountain and Pond are four miles northeast of Saranac Lake and three miles southeast of Bloomingdale. Prior mountain names appearing on earlier maps were Slide, Moose Pond, and on a 1904 United States Geological Survey map, just Moose.

More than fifty geographic features in the Adirondack Park have the moose name on them. Moose disappeared in the nineteenth century but more recently have made a comeback.

MORGAN MOUNTAIN

U.S.G.S. ELEVATION 3432 ft. (H.H.)

High Peaks Region, Essex County, Town of Wilmington

One might think that this mountain was for Edwin D. Morgan, 21st Governor of New York State, or perhaps John Pierpont Morgan, a well-known industrialist in American History and an Adirondack landowner. However, neither is the case.

According to the *Wilmington Town Ledger* (1821-1865), the Morgan family lived in Wilmington. Edward Morgan, in the early founding of Wilmington, in 1824 was a path-master, a public official in charge of road construction and repair. Each property owner had to service all the road-ways on their property. Edward later became one of three Wilmington Commissioners of Highways who oversaw the 14 pathmasters.

According to the Wilmington Tax Assessment Records of 1850-1869, Parker Morgan, the next-door neighbor to Edward Morgan, could have been his father or brother. Parker owned 120 acres of land likely near or adjacent to current day Morgan Mountain.

N-ORONYMS

"Far above the chilly waters of Lake Avalanche, at an elevation of 4,293 feet...is a minute, unpretending tear of the clouds-as it were-a lonely pool shivering in the breezes of the mountains, and sending its limpid surplus through Feldspar Brook to the Opalescent River, the well-spring of the Hudson."

—— **VERPLANCK COLVIN** ——
Surveyor (referring to Lake Tear
of the Clouds, the highest source of the Hudson)

NIPPLETOP

U.S.G.S. ELEVATION 4554 ft. (H.H.)

High Peaks Region, Essex County, Town of Keene

Again, this was a mountain named for its characteristic shape by Old Mountain Phelps. Author Edwin Wallace in his book, *Descriptive Guide to the Adirondacks...,* stated, "Nippletop derived its name from the curious elevation rising from the center of its dome-shaped summit. This mountain was formerly known as Dial."[20]

NOONMARK MOUNTAIN

U.S.G.S. ELEVATION 3491 ft. (H.H.)

High Peaks Region, Essex County, Town of Keene

This mountain is probably one of the world's largest clocks for the residents of Keene Valley. When the sun appears vertically over the summit, it marks Noon. A nearby

20   Edwin R. Wallace. *Descriptive guide to the Adirondacks: land of the thousand lakes and to Saratoga Springs; Schroon Lake; lakes Luzerne, George, and Champlain; the Ausable chasm; Massena Springs; and Trenton Falls.* (Syracuse, N.Y., W. Gill, 1894). Accessed July 29, 2014. https://archive.org/details/descriptiveguide00walluoft, 342.

famous eatery, Noonmark Diner, visited by locals and hikers, was named for the nearby mountain.

Noonmark has the famed Henry L. Stimson Trail on it. Stimson, who first scouted the trail, served as Secretary of State under President Hoover and Secretary of War under President Franklin D. Roosevelt.

≫→

NORTH RIVER MOUNTAINS
U.S.G.S. ELEVATION 2884 ft. (H.H.)
High Peaks Region, Essex County, Town of Newcomb

The Hudson River was once called the North River by the Dutch. They gave this body of water this name as it was north of their settlement of New Amsterdam (New York City).

The North River Mountains, situated very close to the northern source of the Hudson River, was probably named after the earlier name for this river.

≫→

NYE MOUNTAIN
U.S.G.S. ELEVATION 3871 ft. (H.H.)
High Peaks Region, Essex County, Town of North Elba

William B. Nye or Bill Nye (1816-1893) of North Elba was Verplanck Colvin's favorite guide. So, Colvin had a trailless peak named after him.

With Verplanck Colvin, Nye discovered the source of the Hudson River, which Colvin named the source Lake

Tear-of-the-Clouds. The former names of this lake were Summit Lake, Summit Water, and Perkins Pond. Nye also was known for the first ascent, with Verplanck Colvin of Gray Peak.

William Nye, born in Berlin, Vermont, was not always a guide. As a young lad of 19, he yearned for the sea. He worked on a whaling vessel and other boats operated by slaves out of Charlestown Harbor, South Carolina.

Later in 1852, on the west branch of the Ausable River, he built a sawmill. Following this venture, he became a guide.

In the springtime, when Nye was not guiding, he could be found running his sugar works at the farm near Lake Placid of his good friend, abolitionist John Brown. History remembers John Brown for his 1859 raid on a federal armory and arsenal in Harper's Ferry (Harpers Ferry), Virginia, where he was tried for treason and hung.

Bill Nye passed away at age 77 after a burning candle in his room started a fire.

P-ORONYMS

"Everything depends, in the Adirondacks, as in so many other regions of life, upon your guide..."

—— **HENRY VAN DYKE** ——

American Educator, Diplomat, Clergyman and Author of *Little Rivers*

P

PANTHER MOUNTAIN

U.S.G.S. ELEVATION 3763 ft. (H.H.)

Central Region, Hamilton County, Town of Indian Lake

(See Panther Peak)

PANTHER PEAK

U.S.G.S. ELEVATION 4455 ft. (H.H.)

High Peaks Region, Essex County, Town of Newcomb

Panthers were said to be in abundance in the early Adirondacks but became scarce during Verplanck Colvin's Adirondack Survey and no longer present by the end of the 1900s.

Topographical features bearing the word panther in it are commonplace throughout the Adirondacks. In other parts of the United States, the panther is referred to as a mountain lion, puma, catamount, painter, or cougar. Panther Peak and Panther Mountain above bear this animal's name.

PHELPS MOUNTAIN

U.S.G.S. ELEVATION 4137 ft. (H.H.)

High Peaks Region, Essex County, Town of North Elba

Orson Schofield (Old Mountain) Phelps (1816-1905) was probably the most famous of all Adirondack guides. Authors Charles Dudley Warner, E. R. Wallace, and the photography of Seneca Ray Stoddard made him a legend and a household name.

Phelps was born in Vermont, and with his parents and siblings, Orson Phelps moved to Schroon Lake in 1830. Old Mountain Phelps worked for the McIntyre Iron Works (mine) until the accidental death of David Henderson (Henderson Mountain). After this job, he became a guide and mountain climber in Keene Valley.

As a mountain climber, Phelps was the first to climb many of the Adirondack mountains, including Mount Marcy

Old Mountain Phelps
Courtesy of Adirondack Research Library

(1849), which he called Mercy Mountain and named many of the peaks in the Adirondacks after people and shapes. He helped to name Haystack, Basin, Saddleback, Skylight, and the Gothics. Verplanck Colvin, whom Phelps guided for many times, called a peak in his name.

Besides being a guide, Phelps dabbled in other endeavors, such as starting the first postal service in Keene Valley. He carried the mail for free for six months until the federal government took over deliveries. As a writer, he wrote several articles for the *Essex County Republican* newspaper from 1870-75. Phelps was instrumental in coming up with an agreement with the Thomas and Armstrong Lumber Company that allowed guides to build camps on their property, and Phelps was one of the first to construct a dwelling.

He sold Stoddard photographs, guidebooks, trail maps, and even a Phelps-model fishing pole to make extra money.

Old Mountain Phelps died at 88 in his beloved Keene Valley. Many authors have summed up Old Mountain Phelps' importance to the region and the people he guided. In 1902, Harry V. Radford, Adirondack Murray's biographer, wrote, "Phelps was undoubtedly the greatest mountaineer this region has produced and had earned the name "Old Mountain" for his ability to seek out the easiest and most accessible routes to the most lofty and rugged summits in the state."[21]

Charles Dudley Warner, a famous essayist and an author during Phelps's time, made Phelps famous in his writings and compared him to the great philosopher, Socrates. Warner said of Phelps, "Phelps took people to his mountains. When they went home, they had a greater appreciation of their experience than merely the view they'd seen. He was a teacher, philosopher, and the most famous guide."[22]

---

21 Brumley, *Guides of the Adirondack*, 150.

22 Brumley, *Guides of the Adirondack*, 365.

Russell Carson summed up Old Mountain Phelps in his 1927 book, *Peaks and People of the Adirondacks.* "He was a great guide because, in addition to a guide's equipment of woodcraft and knowledge of topography, he had the soul of a philosopher and poet and a fine appreciation of the beauties and sublimities of nature…"[23]

PILLSBURY MOUNTAIN
U.S.G.S. ELEVATION 3589 ft. (H.H.) F.T.
Central Region, Hamilton County, Town of Arietta

Captain Louis Dwight "L.D." Pilsbury (yes, spelled with one "l") and his friend and guide, Whitney, were the first people to carry boats across what are known today as Pillsbury and Whitney Lakes. According to author Edwin Wallace, Pillsbury Mountain and Pillsbury Lake were so-called for L.D. Pilsbury (1832-1906). L.D Pilsbury became the first Superintendent of New York State Prisons.

PITCHOFF MOUNTAIN
U.S.G.S. ELEVATION 3501 ft. (H.H.)
High Peaks Region, Essex County, Town of Keene

In his book, *The Indian Pass,* Alfred Street writes, "Pitchoff Mountain derived its name from a leaning rock of 500 feet at the northeast corner of its crest".[24]

23   Carson, *Peaks and People of the Adirondacks,* 209.

24   Alfred B Street. *The Indian Pass.* Accessed January 26, 2020. archive.org/details/indianpass00sterich/page/n6/mode/2up.

PORTER MOUNTAIN
U.S.G.S. ELEVATION 4068 ft. (H.H.)
High Peaks Region, Essex County, Town of Keene

Dr. Noah Thomas Porter (1811-1892), President of Yale University, made the first ascent of West Mountain with his guide, Ed Phelps (Old Mountain Phelps' son). People knew Porter as an experienced woodsman, oarsman, and untiring walker. Initially, West Mountain, Porter Mountain, honored the man who made the first ascent of the mountain in 1875 with guide Ed Phelps.

PROSPECT MOUNTAIN
U.S.G.S. ELEVATION 2018 ft.
Southeastern Region, Warren County, Town of Lake George

This mountain was first named Prospect Mountain. One of the meanings of prospect is a broad view. Many hikers and visitors have commented on the unobstructed views from Prospect Mountain's summit.

Thomas Reeves Lord's book, *More Stories of Lake George, Fact and Fancy*, described a hiker's diary notation regarding Prospect Mountain. "This afternoon, we climbed a tall alp (Prospect Mountain) south of Caldwell (the original name for today's Lake George Village) for an unobstructed view of Lake George. the way was strenuous, and we toiled many long hours to reach the summit. When our objective was finally reached, it was found to be a place- where to the north, pine trees in prospect rise; -where to the east, pine trees assail the skies; where to the west, pine trees obstruct the river; where to the south, pine trees forever grew!"[25]

---

25   Thomas Reeves Lord. *More Stories of Lake George, Fact and Fancy*. (Pemberton, New Jersey: Pinelands Press, 1994), 28.

Prospect Mountain's name was later changed to Mount Ferguson when Dr. James Ferguson of Glens Falls purchased it in 1877. There Dr. Ferguson built a hotel named the Mount Ferguson House on the site where there had been a log cabin. He wanted his dwelling to house tuberculosis patients, but a hotel became preferable. The Ferguson House soon burned to the ground caused by a forest fire that started by clearing some land nearby that grew out of control.

The next entrepreneur of Prospect Mountain (named changed back to Prospect) was William Peck. He built another hotel on its crest. In 1895, Mr. Peck, along with the Horicon Improvement Company and the Otis Engineering Company, built the world's first and most significant inclined railway up the mountain. After a few years, the railway lost its popularity.

In 1904, George Foster Peabody, an American banker, and philanthropist purchased Prospect Mountain and later deeded the land to New York State. New York State built a road up Prospect Mountain's summit to carry travelers up the mountain by car. The road is still in operation today.

PUFFER MOUNTAIN
U.S.G.S. ELEVATION 3438 ft. (H.H.)
Northern Region, Warren County, Town of Johnsburg

Puffer Mountain could have received its name from a nearby pond or for Thomas Puffer, an Adirondack guide or a landowner.

ROCKY PEAK RIDGE, Giant's wife, by Kay Flickinger
Courtesy of Adirondack Research Library

R-ORONYMS

*"Every mountain top is within reach
if you just keep climbing."*

—— **BARRY FINLAY** ——
Canadian Author

MOUNT REDFIELD

U.S.G.S. ELEVATION 4603 ft. (H.H.)

High Peaks Region, Essex County, Town of Keene

Verplanck Colvin named Mount Redfield for William C. Redfield (1789-1857) for his many contributions to science in America. Redfield was a well-known meteorologist, geologist, and explorer of the Adirondacks.

ROCKY PEAK RIDGE

U.S.G.S. ELEVATION 4193 ft. (H.H.)

High Peaks Region, Essex County, Town of Keene

This peak initially appeared on earlier maps as Bald Peak and Rock Peak. This mountain had a series of fires on it. Its rocky and barren appearance has given its name Rocky Peak Ridge.

Rocky Peak Ridge is often referred to as "Giant's (mountain) Wife" because it is located right next to Giant and shorter than Giant.

S-ORONYMS

*"It is human nature to stretch, to go, to see, to understand.
Exploration is not a choice, really: it's an imperative."*

—— **MICHAEL COLLINS** ——

Apollo 11 Command Module Pilot Astronaut

S

SADDLEBACK MOUNTAIN
U.S.G.S. ELEVATION 4534 ft. (H.H.)
High Peaks Region, Essex County, Town of Keene

As they viewed the mountain from Mount Marcy, Frederick S. Perkins, an Adirondack painter, and Old Mountain Phelps called the mountain, Saddleback for its saddle-like shape. Perkins spent many summers painting in the Adirondacks, and he and Phelps named many of these mountains.

SADDLEBACK MOUNTAIN
U.S.G.S. ELEVATION 3560 ft. (H.H.)
Northern Region, Essex County, Town of Lewis

This mountain has a characteristic saddle shape because of its two bumps on this mountain.

SAINT REGIS MOUNTAIN
U.S.G.S. ELEVATION 2838 ft. (S.S.) FT
Northern Region, Franklin County, Town of Santa Clara

St. Regis Mountain, located 14.6 miles from Saranac Lake, is one of the Saranac Six Mountains. Its bare rock summit is due to a fire started accidentally by Verplanck Colvin's surveying party.

St. Regis Mountain, along with all waterways, towns, etc. bearing the name St. Regis, were named for Father Jean Francois Regis (1597-1640), a French clergyman. He advocated for the laboring class and hoped to be a missionary for the Iroquois. Unfortunately, before completing his goals, he died at the young age of 43. Pope Clement XII canonized and proclaimed him the patron saint of lacemakers, medical social workers, and illegitimate children in 1737.

St. Regis, like some other Adirondack and Catskill Mountains, has a fire tower at its summit. The Friends of St. Regis Fire Tower refurbished the over hundred-year fire tower. An observer would stay on the mountain to spot forest fires until airplanes replaced fire towers and its observers. To pay tribute to these observers for the past years, volunteers from the Friends of St. Regis Fire Tower have climbed the mountain and lit the tower cab from 9:00 to 9:30 pm, usually on the last Saturday night in August.

SANTANONI PEAK
U.S.G.S. ELEVATION 4596 ft. (H.H.)
High Peaks Region, Essex County, Town of Newcomb

The name of this peak originated from the Abenaki corruption of the French Saint Antoine for Saint Anthony. The Native Americans called it "Great Mountain." It first appeared on a William Redfield map in 1838.

SAWTEETH

U.S.G.S. ELEVATION 4114 ft. (H.H.)

High Peaks Region, Essex County, Town of Keene

Originally called Resagonia by Reverend Erastus Hopkins of Northampton, Massachusetts, Resagonia was an Italian word meaning the "king's great saw." Early geologists called it Sawtooth (mountain), but at a glance, they noticed a series of notches lined up like the teeth of a saw. So, it was called Sawteeth (mountain).

In 1875, Yale University student Newell Martin, a Yale University student, was the first to climb Sawteeth because of its ruggedness.

SAWTOOTH MOUNTAINS

U.S.G.S. ELEVATION 3402 ft. (H.H.)

High Peaks Region, Franklin County, Town of Harrietstown

Sawtooth Mountain 1 and Sawtooth Mountains 2, 3, 4, and 5 that follow have knobs on top and descend in altitude.

SCARFACE MOUNTAIN

U.S.G.S. ELEVATION 3058 ft. (S.S.)

High Peaks Region, Essex County, Town of North Elba

Scarface is one of the Saranac Six Mountains. Scarface most likely received its name from the open rock slab on the north side, observed from many vantage points in the Ray Brook and the Saranac Lake Region. The early Native Americans viewed the mountain in the same way. They had a name for it in their language.

Before being called Scarface, it was called Rogers Mountain. It still is by some locals. Rogers Mountain was owned and logged by J. &J. Rogers Lumber Company. However, the lumber company had to give up the mountain to pay its back taxes. Eventually, it became state land and a "Forever Wild" forest.

Scarface was in the news early in Adirondack history when Godfrey Dewey, son of Melvil Dewey, and others worked on the 1932 Lake Placid Winter Olympics. In June 1929, Godfrey and other organizers secured permission from the New York State Department of Conservation and the landowner to build the bobsled course for the games there. Then the effort was shot down as unconstitutional by the Association for the Protection of the Adirondacks. One could not cut on New York State land under the Forever Wild clause of the New York State Constitution. With the games in jeopardy, Godfrey Dewey donated land around North Meadow Ridge to the Town of North Elba for a bobsled run. He renamed the land Mount Van Hoevenberg in honor of his old hiking buddy, Henry Van Hoevenberg.

Scarface Mountain made international news in January 2014. An Australian soldier, Paul McKay, flew 12,000 miles from his home in Canberra, Australia. He rented a car, drove to the village of Saranac Lake, hiked up Scarface, sat down, and died from hypothermia. Captain McKay had post-traumatic stress disorder (P.T.S.D.), caused by experiencing shocking events in the Afghanistan war zone. Soon after, searchers located his body.

What followed was an intense outpouring of support between Australia, Saranac Lake, and the rest of the world brought through social media. The mayor of Saranac Lake, Clyde Rabideau, and others held a memorial service for the young soldier. The good that came out of this sad event was educating more people about P.T.S.D. for our soldiers returning from war zones.

SENTINEL MOUNTAIN

U.S.G.S. ELEVATION 3835 ft. (H.H.)

High Peaks Region, Essex County, Town of Wilmington

Sentinel and its range are close to Lake Placid's village, but they are the least known wilderness areas in the Adirondack Park. It is a prominent landmark from New York State's Route 9N.

Verplanck Colvin and his Adirondack Survey Crew did not visit the peaks in this area until late in Colvin's career, and in 1895 Colvin Adirondack guide Rod McKenzie first climbed Sentinel to build a signal on its summit.

The original manuscripts of Old Mountain Phelps housed at the Adirondack Research Library at the Kelly Adirondack Center of Union College in Niskayuna, New York, conveyed that John Fitch named Sentinel. Colvin stated, "The Sentinel Range, as seen from the Northward, appears like a single sharp peak-a vidette of the great army of mountains at the headwaters of the Ausable. From its solitary appearance it is supposed it looked like a single guard."[26]

---

26   ___ Manuscript, *The Adirondacks,* undated, Box 1, Folder 19, ARL-051, Orson Schofield Phelps collection, Adirondack Research Library, Union College.

Phelps also makes another reference about Sentinel in that he states, "This is an interesting group… has a number of high summits including the Sentinel summit which makes out well to the east branch nearer the line of Keene and Jay. It was named from its prominent (sic) look over the East Valley."[27]

》——▶

SEWARD MOUNTAIN
U.S.G.S. ELEVATION 4327 ft. (H.H.)
High Peaks Region, Franklin County, Town of Harrietstown

This mountain was for the 12th New York State Governor, William Henry Seward (1839-1842), who succeeded Governor Marcy.

William Seward (1801-1872) was born in Florida, New York, Orange County. There his father farmed and owned slaves. In 1801, William Seward graduated from Union College in Schenectady, New York, with a B.A.

Following his education at Union, he made Auburn, New York, his home and practiced law there. His career in law led him to an interest in politics. He served in the New York State Senate from 1830 until 1834 and was elected Governor of New York in 1838 and 1840 and serving two consecutive terms. While governor, he did much to promote Black residents' rights as citizens and did much for the abolitionists.

As a United States Senator representing New York State from March 4, 1849 - March 3, 1861, he started the Republican Party. In 1861, he became Secretary of State for President Lincoln and served in that post for President Andrew Johnson upon Lincoln's assassination.

---

27   Manuscript, *The Adirondacks.*

SEWARD MOUNTAIN named for William Seward
who purchased Alaska, by Kay Flickinger
Courtesy of Adirondack Research Library

In American history, Seward negotiated the purchase of Alaska from Russia when he was U.S. Secretary of State under President Andrew Johnson. Many people felt that the sum of 7.2 million dollars was way too much to pay for Alaska since it was barren and unexplored. This purchase received such nicknames as "Seward's Folly," "Seward's Icebox," and "Polar Bear Garden." However, history would prove those people wrong.

Seward was active throughout his life as an abolitionist. He died at his home in Auburn, New York.

SEYMOUR MOUNTAIN

U.S.G.S. ELEVATION 4055 ft. (H.H.)

High Peaks Region, Franklin County, Town of Harrietstown

Unlike most other governors of New York State, Horatio Seymour (1810-1886) explored the Adirondack region several times per year during different seasons. These visits greatly impressed surveyor Verplanck Colvin.

Horatio Seymour was born in Pompey Hill, Onondaga, New York. At the age of ten, he moved with his family to Utica, New York. He attended several local schools and Geneva College (now Hobart College), followed by the American Literary, Scientific & Military (now Norwich University) Academy.

After a brief career in law, Seymour became interested in politics. In 1833, he began his service as military secretary to Governor William Learned Marcy for six years. Later, Seymour went on to serve as a member of the New York State Assembly. At the same time, he was doing a term as mayor of Utica. Seymour served two terms as governor but not consecutively.

After serving New York State in his many capacities, Seymour went on to run for President of the United States against Ulysses S. Grant in the Election of 1868. Although the popular vote was close, the electoral vote was not, and Seymour returned to private life to help to rebuild the Democratic Party. He died in Utica.

MOUNT SKYLIGHT

U.S.G.S. ELEVATION 4908 ft. (H.H.)

High Peaks Region, Essex County, Town of Keene

In 1857, Adirondack Guide Old Mountain Phelps and Frederick S. Perkins climbed Mount Marcy. The top of Mount Marcy provided such a view of the surrounding peaks that they started giving these peaks names. One side of one summit looked to them like a dormer window on the roof, so they named it Mount Skylight.

Verplanck Colvin and his survey crew would be the first to climb Mount Skylight in 1873.

Mount Skylight's rocky summit provides beautiful views of the area for climbers. Hikers have established a custom of carrying a small stone to the top. They believe failure to do so will cause a rainstorm to occur for the hikers.

SLIDE MOUNTAIN

U.S.G.S. ELEVATION 3586 ft. (H.H.)

High Peaks Region, Essex County, Town of Keene

Slide Mountain's name would imply that there was a slide on it at one time. Located at the corner of Keene, Wilmington, and North Elba townships, Slide Mountain is trailless.

SNOWY MOUNTAIN

U.S.G.S. ELEVATION 3825 ft. (H.H.) F.T.

Central Region, Hamilton County, Town of Indian Lake

Snowy, "The Mount Marcy of the Southern Adirondacks," as it is known, is a very popular climb for hikers.

Colvin first climbed Snowy Mountain on August 3 and 4, 1872. Colvin said in a report to the State Legislature, "We immediately addressed ourselves to the ascent and early in the day reached the summit of the peak (mountain) which I shall hereafter term "Snowy Mountain…is known to guides and hunters as Bald Face or Snowy Mountain (the snow remaining on it late in the spring and has several other titles.)."[28]

Past names given to this mountain were Squaw Bonnet, Devil's Ear, and Lake Lewey Mountain.

---

28   Colvin. *Report on the Topographical Survey,* 1873.

SOUTH DIX

U.S.G.S. ELEVATION 4088 ft. (H.H.)

High Peaks Region, Essex County, Town of North Hudson

South Dix is just another mountain named for John Dix, a past governor of New York State. You can read more about John Dix in the entry for Dix Mountain.

STEWART MOUNTAIN

U.S.G.S. ELEVATION 3602 ft. (H.H.)

High Peaks Region, Essex County, Town of Wilmington

Stewart Mountain might have acquired its name from settlers who inhabited the land nearby where this mountain is situated, like Kilburn and Morgan Mountains.

STREET MOUNTAIN

U.S.G.S. ELEVATION 4022 ft. (H.H.)

High Peaks Region, Essex County, Town of North Elba

Alfred Billings Street (1811-1881) practiced law in Monticello and Albany, New York. In 1848 he was named the New York State Law Librarian, a post he held until his death.

Aside from being a lawyer, he was a man of many talents. He was an author and poet. Alfred Street is best known for his book, *The Indian Pass*, his 1869 journey through the Adirondacks to visit four gorges and other geographical features. His poetry dealt with the natural world and the life and times of primitive America.

SUNRISE MOUNTAIN
U.S.G.S. ELEVATION 3606 ft. (H.H.)
High Peaks Region, Essex County, Town of North Hudson

No research was found that suggests the origin of the mountain's name. Its elevated summit does provide for a panoramic view and could provide for a beautiful sunrise.

T-ORONYMS

"When you go to the mountains, you see them, and you admire them. In a sense, they give you a challenge, and you try to express that challenge by climbing them..."

—— SIR EDMUND HILLARY ——

New Zealand Mountaineer

T R MOUNTAIN

U.S.G.S. ELEVATION 3829 ft. (H.H.)

High Peaks Region, Essex County, Town of Keene

In 1999, New York Governor, George Pataki, renamed this mountain for Theodore (Teddy) Roosevelt (1858-1919). T R Mountain, formerly known as Indian Falls Peak, was renamed during the yearly held Teddy Roosevelt Days in Newcomb, New York.

Theodore Roosevelt was no stranger to the Adirondacks. As a young boy, Teddy spent three summers in the Adirondacks studying birds and becoming an ornithologist. He even wrote a book with his Harvard classmate, Henry Davis Minot in 1877 entitled, *The Summer Birds of the Adirondacks in Franklin County, N. Y.*

In the Spanish American War, Roosevelt served and led his famous Rough Riders in Cuba in the Battle of San Juan Hill in an American victory. Because of his war-hero status, he was easily elected Governor of New York State in the election of 1898.

After one term as governor, he became Vice-President of the United States under President William McKinley. On September 6, 1901, President McKinley was in Buffalo, New York, attending the Pan American Exposition. It was there that Leon Czolgosz, an anarchist, shot him. While vacationing on Lake Champlain, Roosevelt was notified and went to Buffalo.

Roosevelt stayed in Buffalo until McKinley was out of danger and rejoined his family for a vacation in the Adirondacks. They were a guest of James MacNaughton at the Tahawus Club.

One of the activities for Roosevelt while at the Tahawus Club was to climb Mount Marcy. Roosevelt climbed to the top of Mount Marcy on September 13 but only stayed there fifteen minutes due to a rainstorm. Roosevelt and family descended Marcy and reached Lake Tear of the Clouds, the source of the Hudson. While enjoying their lunch, a messenger arrived with communication. McKinley had taken a turn for the worse and was dying.

Roosevelt and his company ran down the rest of the mountain and reached the Tahawus Club.

At 11:00 pm, another message arrived that McKinley's condition was dire. After the communication, Roosevelt began his journey in an open buckboard to the North Creek train station to travel to Buffalo. The ride was dark, rutty, and muddy- a very uncomfortable ride. It took three drivers and three sets of horses for the trek.

At 2:15 am on September 14, President McKinley passed away during Mr. Roosevelt's first journey leg. John Cronin, Roosevelt's driver, knew Theodore Roosevelt had become President but decided not to tell him. Cronin feared it might create more anxiety for Roosevelt's already wild ride. A historical marker on the road between Newcomb and Minerva, New York, was later erected on the site where Theodore Roosevelt became president.

At the Aiden Lair Hotel, owned by Cronin, they made a pit stop to change horses. Cronin tried to convince Roosevelt to stay at Aiden Lair until early the following day, but Roosevelt wanted to keep going.

They arrived in North Creek later that day. Via a telegram from United States Secretary of State John Hay, Theodore Roosevelt learned he had become the 26th president. The rest is history.

In the polls of the most famous American presidents, Theodore Roosevelt is almost always in the top five. Roosevelt's sculptured face and George Washington, Abraham Lincoln, and Thomas Jefferson make up the Mount Rushmore National Memorial in Black Hills National Forest in South Dakota.

TABLE TOP MOUNTAIN
U.S.G.S. ELEVATION 4295 ft. (H.H.)
High Peaks Region, Essex County, Town of Keene

From other mountains, this summit is viewed as flat and depicted as the top of a table. Both Verplanck Colvin and Old Mountain Phelps often referred to it as Flattop Mountain. In 1876 in O.W. Gray's *New Topographical Atlas of Essex County, New York...* it was labeled Table Top Mountain.

U-ORONYMS

"One day's exposure to mountains
is better than a cartload of books."

—— JOHN MUIR ——
Naturalist and Author

U

UNNAMED PEAK
(BROWN POND), ELEVATION 3419 ft. (H.H.)
Central Region, Hamilton County, Town of Indian Lake

This unnamed peak is known as Brown Pond to locals and hikers, as its namesake lies on the western slope. Its watercolor or settlers with a Brown surname nearby could have contributed to its name.

UNNAMED PEAK
(LOST POND), ELEVATION 3900 ft. (H.H.)
High Peaks Region, Essex County, Town of North Elba

In 1929, George Marshall and his guide, Herb Clark, climbed this mountain calling this mountain well-named. This toponym, like Brown Pond, is named by locals and has not yet been accepted by United States Board on Geographic Names. Lost Pond, the fifth-highest New York State water body, lies near this unnamed mountain's summit or peak.

UPPER WOLFJAW MOUNTAIN

U.S.G.S. ELEVATION 4185 ft. (H.H.)

High Peaks Region, Essex County, Town of Keene

(See Lower Wolfjaw)

V-ORONYMS

"FOR THE SHEER JOY OF CLIMBING."

Words inscribed on a plaque on Esther Mountain honoring the spirit of Esther McComb, the peak's namesake. It was placed there by the Adirondack Forty-Sixers organization in 1939.

V

MOUNT VAN HOEVENBERG

U.S.G.S. ELEVATION 2923 ft.

High Peaks Region, Essex County, Town of North Elba

Henry Van Hoevenberg (1849-1918), born in Oswego, New York, grew up in Troy. New York. He became a self-taught electrical engineer and worked in New York City. Also, he was an inventor and a successful telegraph operator, having several patents in telegraphy.

Henry was looking for a different place to spend his summer vacation rather than in New York City and where he could escape his hay fever. He decided to camp in the Adirondacks. It was there near Upper Ausable Lake in 1877 that he met his sweetheart, Josephine Schofield, from Brooklyn, New York. They hit it off and found themselves engaged. As Henry and Josephine stood on the summit of Mount Marcy one day, they eyed a spot for their home. Their home was beside a water body that would later be named Heart Lake because of its shape. Henry named a nearby mountain after Josephine and called it Mount Jo.

They would never realize the dream of a shared mountain home. Josephine's father called her home when learning of this love affair. He told her she could not marry Henry, because he was not Jewish. Josephine then died a mysterious death. Henry never got over the loss of Jo and never married.

Despite the loss of his beloved Josephine, Henry, "Van" or "The Man in Leather" as he was known, still went on to build a magnificent Adirondack lodge. He built on the site that he and Jo had picked out for their home. His close friend, Godfrey Dewey, son of Melvil Dewey, called Henry's log hotel one of the best in the whole world. At the time, it was the largest log structure in the United States. It was also one of the first hotels with private baths. Henry operated the lodge from 1880-1898 until he faced financial difficulties. Because of these difficulties, Henry sold the Adirondack Lodge to the Lake Placid Company, owner of the Lake Placid Club, founded by Melville (Melvil) Dewey and his wife, Annie.

Henry Van Hoevenberg would manage the Adirondack Lodge for the Lake Placid Club until a forest fire in 1903 destroyed the lodge. Henry continued to work for the Lake Placid Club until his death.

A new lodge was built in 1927. Melvil Dewey changed the name of the Adirondack Lodge to Adirondack Loj for its phonetic spelling. Later, it became just The Loj.

Dr. Melvil Dewey, a native of Adams Center, near Watertown, New York, was the "The Father of Modern Library Science." He originated the library classification system known as the Dewey Decimal System and was the New York State Librarian. He would later be instrumental in securing the 1932 Olympic Games for Lake Placid. Dewey also started a Lake Placid Club in Florida in Lake Stearns, later renamed Lake Placid, Florida. Melvil Dewey died of a stroke in 1931 in Lake Placid, Florida.

In 1957, the Lake Placid Club sold it to the Adirondack Mountain Club. The Loj provided for the lodging of its members and guests and offered activities. Mount Van Hoevenberg became an Olympic venue in 1932 for the bobsleigh and 1980 Olympics bobsleigh and luge competitions.

W-ORONYMS

"Mountains are earth's undecaying monuments...."

NATHANIEL HAWTHORNE
American Author

WAKELY MOUNTAIN

U.S.G.S. ELEVATION 3750 ft. (H.H.) F.T.

Central Region, Hamilton County, Town of Lake Pleasant

British-born William D. Wakeley was a hotelkeeper in Cedar River Falls, New York. He had only received three months of formal education; however, he knew enough math to succeed in business.

An advertisement in *Wallace's Guide to the Adirondacks of 1878* portrays Wakeley's hotel as having the finest hunting grounds in the Adirondacks.

The United States Geological Survey approved the mountain for William D. Wakeley, but the United States Geological Survey omitted the "e" in Wakeley's name.

WALLFACE MOUNTAIN

U.S.G.S. ELEVATION 3720 ft. (H.H.)

High Peaks Region, Essex County, Town of North Elba

According to Historian Alfred Donaldson, "Wallface presents an almost vertical precipice of naked rock. At many places in this deep abyss, the ice never melts, and rays of the sun never shine."[29] Ebenezer Emmons was the first to climb this mountain in 1838 and dubbed it Wall-face, for the cliff looked like a wall and face.

WHITEFACE MOUNTAIN

U.S.G.S. ELEVATION 4816 ft. (H.H.)

High Peaks Region, Essex County, Town of Wilmington

Horatio Gates Spafford first named the mountain, Whiteface in his book, *A Gazetteer of the State of New-York*, published in 1813.

Professor Ebeneezer, in a New York State Assembly document, explained Whiteface. "Whiteface is a high mountain in the north part of Essex County, which receives its name from the circumstance of a slide having, on one side, laid bare the rock, which has a grayish white appearance."[30]

Whiteface, the most famous Adirondack mountain, witnessed skiing competitions for the 1932 and 1980 Olympics. As a result, this mountain became known as "The Olympic Mountain."

In 1929, Franklin Delano Roosevelt (F.D.R.), then Governor of New York State, started a project to build a highway up the mountain dedicated to World War I veterans. Later, when he was President of the United States, he would dedicate the road to the World War I veterans.

In 1961, Whiteface Mountain became a field site for the State University of New York's living lab. Dr. Vincent Schae-

---

29   Donaldson, *The History of the Adirondacks,* 1:164.

30   Carson, *Peaks and People of the Adirondacks,* 17.

View of surrouding peaks from NYS WHITEFACE MOUNTAIN
Ski Trail, Mid 20th Century, by Monroe Dixson
Courtesy of Richard Dixson

New York State WHITEFACE MOUNTAIN Chairlift,
Mid 20th Century, by Monroe Dixson

Courtesy of Richard Dixson

fer, was instrumental in creating this lab. He was a chemist, meteorologist, and researcher for General Electric (G.E.), in Schenectady, New York. Dr. Schaefer had several patents and developed cloud seedings. His staff included Atmospheric Scientist Bernie Vonnegut, Meteorologist Ray Falconer, and others. This became known as ASRC (Atmospheric Science Research Center) Whiteface Mountain Field Station.

Scientists from all parts of the world would come to study chemistry, acid rain, red spruce decline, etc. at the atmospheric center. Many weather forecasts were also delivered from its location.

Mario Cuomo, Governor of New York State, in 1985, would rededicate it to veterans of all United States wars. A memorial plaque was placed on the mountain to honor the Army's 10th Mountain Division. They were the ski troops who fought in Italy and Alaska's Aleutian Islands during World War II. Following World War II, these ski soldiers, like Hal Burton (Burtons Peak), helped build ski resorts at Whiteface, Vail, and other resorts throughout the United States.

Whiteface is also known as one of three ski mountains owned and operated by New York State. The other two are Gore Mountain in the Adirondacks and Belleayre Mountain in the Catskills.

WOLF POND MOUNTAIN
U.S.G.S. ELEVATION 3425 ft. (H.H.)

Central Region, Essex County, Town of North Hudson

This pond and mountain were appropriately named. Wolves frequently visited groups of people camping in the area of this pond and mountain.

WRIGHT PEAK
U.S.G.S. ELEVATION 4564 ft. (H.H.)
High Peaks Region, Essex County, Town of North Elba

Governor Silas Wright (1795-1847) was born in Amherst, Massachusetts, and graduated from Middlebury College in Vermont. His career included many vocations, including being a lawyer, a New York State Comptroller, Governor of New York State, Brigadier General in the New York State Militia, and New York Senator. Also, Silas Wright served in both houses of the United States Congress.

Any climber near the summit of Wright Peak will find a memorial plaque. The plaque list members of the Strategic Air Command B-47 crew killed in a crash. Their names were followed by, "A Strategic Air Command B-47 crew killed here 16 January 1962 while on a mission preserving the peace of our nation."[31] The B-47 bomber, based at Plattsburgh Air force Base in Plattsburgh, New York, was on a routine training mission when it crashed on Wright Mountain in a very remote area. After five days, searchers found the crash site with no survivors but debris scattered throughout the region.

---

31 ___ "An Air Force Bomber Crashes into Wright Peak." Accessed May 21, 2021. B-47 Crash in the High Peaks (adirondack-park.net).

BIBLIOGRAPHY

Abbott, Henry. *Fishing Brook.* Accessed January 14, 2019. field1=ocr;q1=Fishing%20Brook;a=srchls;lmt=fthttp://babel.hathitrust.org/cgi/pt?id=uc1.$b259232.

Aber, Ted and Stella Brooks King. *The History of Hamilton County.* Lake Pleasant, NY: Great Wilderness Books, 1965.

___"Adirondack Hundred Highest." Accessed May 13, 2021. https://www.peakbagger.com/list.aspx?lid=5121&cid=21903.

___"An Air Force Bomber Crashes into Wright Peak." Accessed May 21, 2021. B-47 Crash in the High Peaks (adirondack-park.net).

Amodeo, Margaret, Hallie Bond, Carl George, J. Douglas Klein, and Richard E. Tucker. *The Adirondack Chronology.* Accessed February 9, 2020. https://digitalworks.union.edu/cgi/viewcontent.cgi?article=1000&context=arlpublications, 143.

Aprill, Dennis. *Paths Less Traveled: The Adirondack Experience for Walkers, Hikers, and Climbers of All Ages.* Mount Kisco, NY: Pinto Press, 1998.

Arnold, Doug. "Grace Peak: A Personal Reflection." *Adirondack Peeks* 51, no. 2 (Fall 2014): 5.

Barker, Dr. E. Eugene. *The Cloud Splitter*. Albany, NY: Albany Chapter of The Adirondack Mountain Club, Nov-Dec 1948, 10.

Barnett, Lincoln and the Editors of Time-Life Books. *The Ancient Adirondacks: The American Wilderness*. New York: Time Inc., 1974.

Beauchamp, William Martin. *Aboriginal Place Names of New York*. Accessed May 7, 2021. https://archive.org/details/aboriginalplacen00beau.

___. "The Best Hike in Every State." *Outside Online*. Accessed May 5, 2019. https://www.outsideonline.com/2393036/50-best-hikes-us April 20, 2019.

___. "Bob Marshall." Accessed April 25, 2021. https://wilderness.net/learn-about-wilderness/bob-marshall.php.

Brown, Phil, ed. *Bob Marshall in the Adirondacks: Writings of a Pioneering Peak-Bagger, Pond-Hopper and Wilderness Preservationist*. Saranac Lake, NY: Lost Pond Press, 2006.

Brown, Phil. *Longstreet Highroad Guide to the New York Adirondacks*. Atlanta, GA: Longstreet Press Inc., 1999.

Bruhns, Walter C. *An Adirondack Affair: Photography and Poetry of the Waters and Mountains*. Walter C. Bruhns, 1988.

Brumley, Charles. *Guides of the Adirondacks: A History: A Short Season-Hard Work-Low Pay*. Utica, NY: North Country Books, Inc., 1994.

Burnside, James R. *Exploring the 46 Adirondack High Peaks*. Schenectady, NY: High Peaks Press, 1996.

Burt, C.H. *The Opening of the Adirondacks*. New York: Hurd and Houghton, 1865.

Carrington, Henry B. and Robert W. Venables. "The Six Nations of New York: The 1892 United States Census Bulletin." *Documents in American Social History*. Ithaca, NY: Cornell University Press, 1996.

Carson, Russell M.L. *Peaks and People of the Adirondacks*. Glens Falls, NY: The Adirondack Mountain Club, 1973.

Collin, Robert L. "The Adirondack Hundred Highest." *Adirondac* 46, no. 6 (August 1982): 18-19.

Colvin: Hero to the North Woods, directed by Bill Killon. (2016; Bannertree Films), DVD.

Colvin, Verplanck. *Report on the Topographical Survey of the Adirondack Wilderness of New York, for the Year 1873*. Albany, NY: Weed, Parsons & Company Printers, 1874.

Colvin, Verplanck. *Seventh Annual Report on the Progress of the Topographical Survey of the Adirondack Region of New York to the Year 1879*. Albany, NY: Weed, Parsons & Company Printers, 1880.

Davis, Jeremy K. *Lost Ski Areas of the Southern Adirondacks*. Charleston, SC: History Press, 2012.

___ "Death of H.K. Averill." *Plattsburg Sentinel* (Plattsburg, NY), April 2, 1918.

Dedam, Kim Smith. "Andrew Goodman to receive posthumous Medal of Freedom." *Press-Republican* (Plattsburgh, NY), November 12, 2014.

Dedam, Kim Smith. "A tragedy shared: Saranac Lake reaches across the world." *Press-Republican* (Plattsburgh, NY), January 21, 2014.

Delehant, Mike. "Baker family housed the famous author." *Adirondack Daily Enterprise* (Saranac Lake, NY), November 9, 2017.

DeSormo, Maitland C. *Summers on the Saranacs*. Utica, NY: North Country Books, July 1980.

Dibelius, Norman L. *Winter Sports*. Schenectady, NY: The Schenectady Wintersports Club, 1995.

___"Discover Dippikill." Accessed February 2, 2020. http://dippikill.com/about.

Donaldson, Alfred L. *A History of the Adirondacks*. 2 vols. Fleischmanns, NY: Purple Mountain Press, LTD., 1992.

Engel, Robert, and others. *Santanoni: From Japanese Temple to Life at an Adirondack Great Camp*. Keeseville, NY: Adirondack Architectural Heritage, 2000.

Flinn, David. "The Top Ten Adirondack Peaks." *alpinejournal.org*. (April 18, 2009). Accessed July 27, 2017. https://www.alpinejournal.org/research/80-mountain-nostalgia-the-top-ten-adirondack-peaks.

Flynn, Andy, and Friends. *New York's Adirondack Park: A User's Guide*. Saranac Lake, NY: Hungry Bear Publishing, 2013.

Friends of Mt. (Mount) Arab. "History of the Fire Observers on Mt. Arab." Accessed April 24, 2019. http://friendsofmtarab.org/abouthistory.html.

Gallos, Phil. *By Foot in the Adirondacks*. Saranac Lake, NY: Adirondack Publishing Company, Inc., 1972.

Gates, William Preston. *Lake George Hotels & Landings*. Queensbury, NY: WP Gates Publishing, 2010.

Gilborn, Craig. *Adirondack Camps: Homes Away from Home 1850-1950*. Syracuse, NY: The Adirondack Museum/Syracuse University Press, 2000.

Goodwin, Tony and David Thomas-Train, eds. *High Peak Trails*. Lake George, NY: Adirondack Mountain Club, 2012.

Gooley, Lawrence P. *Lyon Mountain: The Tragedy of a Mining Town*. Rutland, VT: Bloated Toe Enterprises, 2004.

Grondahl, Paul. "Dippikill: 50 Years of Our Own Little Walden." Accessed May 4, 2021. https://www.albany.edu/news/campus_news/2005/nov2005/dippikill.shtml.

Harder, Kelsie B., ed. *Illustrated Dictionary of Place Names: United States and Canada*. New York: Van Nostrand Reinhold Company, 1976.

Healy, Bill, ed. *The High Peaks of Essex: The Adirondack Mountains of Orson Schofield Phelps*. Fleischmanns, NY: Purple Mountain Press, 1992.

___. *Heaven Up-h'isted-ness!* Cadyville, NY: Adirondack Forty-Sixers, Inc., 2011.

Heavey, Bill. "High Peaks of the Adirondacks." *National Geographic Traveler*, July, August 1995, 28-39.

Heller, Murray. *Call Me Adirondack: Names and Their Stories*. Saranac Lake, NY: The Chauncy Press, 1989.

___. "Historic New York: The Adirondacks." *The Historical Marker Database*. Accessed April 24, 2019. https://www.hmdb.org/marker.asp?marker=44686.

Hochschild, Harold K. *An Adirondack Resort in the Nineteenth Century Blue Mountain Lake 1870-1900 Stagecoaches and Luxury Hotels*. Blue Mountain Lake, NY: Adirondack Museum, 1962.

Hochschild, Harold K. *The MacIntyre Mine: From Failure to Fortune*. Blue Mountain Lake, NY: Adirondack Museum, 1962.

Hudowalski, Grace L. "Esther." *The Cloudsplitter*, April 1939, 4.

Jamieson, Paul and Neal Burdick, eds. *The Adirondack Reader: Four Centuries of Adirondack Writing*. Lake George, NY: Adirondack Mountain Club, Inc., 2009.

Jenkins, John S. *Lives of the Governors of New York State*. 2 vols. Auburn, NY: Derby & Miller, 1851.

Johnstone, Andrew. "The Loj." *North Country Living Magazine* 5, no. 2 (June/July/August 2016): 8-11, 14, 15.

Kaiser, Harvey H. *Great Camps of the Adirondacks*. Boston: David R. Godine Publisher, Inc., 1982.

Kirschenbaum, Howard, Susan Schafstall and Jeanine Stuchin, eds. *The Adirondack Guide: An Almanac of Essential Information and Assorted Trivia*. Raquette Lake, NY: Sagamore Institute, 1983.

Kopp, Jon. "History of the Fire Observers of Mt Arab." *Friends of Mt Arab*. Accessed July 21, 2017. http://www.friendsofmtarab.org/abouthistory.html.

Lionel Pincus and Princess Firyal Map Division, The New York Public Library. "*New topographical atlas of Essex County, New York: from official records, unpublished maps*

and plans, and special explorations and surveys; with a
supplement comprising a map of the state of New York,
and general maps of the United States and the world, with
descriptions." New York Public Library Digital Collections.
Accessed May 13, 2021. https://digitalcollections.nypl.
org/items/d9f90fa0-c5f7-012f-65e6-58d385a7bc34.

Lord, Thomas Reeves. *More Stories of Lake George, Fact and
Fancy*. Pemberton, NJ: Pinelands Press, 1994.

Ludlum, Stuart D. *Exploring the Adirondack Mountains 100 Years
Ago*. Utica, NY: Brodock & Ludlum Publications, 1972.

___Manuscript, *The Adirondacks*, undated, Box 1, Folder 19,
ARL-051, Orson Schofield Phelps collection, Adirondack
Research Library, Union College.

Marshall, George. "The 3900 Footers." *The Cloudsplitter*. Albany
Chapter of the Adirondack Mountain Club, June 1943.

McMartin, Barbara. *Fifty Hikes in the Adirondacks: Short Walks,
Day Trips, and Backpacks Throughout the Park*. Woodstock,
VT: Backcountry Publications, 1980.

McMartin, Barbara. "The Coney Mountain Story." Kiosk
at the foot of Coney Mountain. Tupper Lake, NY.
Viewed August 17, 2016.

McMartin, Barbara and Bill Ingersoll. *Discover the Central
Adirondacks: Four-Season Adventures in the Heart of the
North Woods*. Canada Lake, NY: Lake View Press, 2002.

McMartin, Barbara and Lee Brenning. *Discover the West
Central Mountains: A Guide to the Western Wildernesses
and the Moose River Plains*. Woodstock, VT:
Backcountry Publications, 1988.

Mellor, Don. *Climbing in the Adirondacks: A Guide to Rock and Ice Routes in the Adirondack Park*. Lake George, NY: Adirondack Mountain Club, 1988.

Morrissey, Spencer. *The Other 54: A Hiker's Guide to the Lower 54 Peaks of the Adirondack 100 Highest*. Lake Placid, NY: Inca-pah-cho Wilderness Guides, 2007.

Murphy, Eloise Cronin. *Theodore Roosevelt's Night Ride to the Presidency*. Blue Mountain Lake, NY: Adirondack Museum, 2008.

Nelson, Pete. "Lost Brook Dispatches: Forever Wild." *The Adirondack Almanack*. April 21, 2012. Accessed January 18, 2017. http:www.adirondackalmanack.com/2012/04/lost-brook-dispatches-forever-wild.html.

Olivero, Antonio. "Seeking 6: Hikers on Tri-Lakes trails enlighten reporter during his pursuit to become a 6er." *Adirondack Daily Enterprise* (Saranac Lake, NY) August 27, 2016, Sec. B: 1.

Pearsall, Glenn C. *When Men and Mountains Meet*. Utica, NY: North Country Books, 2013.

Podskoch, Martin. *Adirondack Fire Towers: Their History and Lore: The Northern Districts*. Fleischmanns, NY: Purple Mountain Press, 2012.

Podskoch, Martin. *Adirondack Fire Towers: Their History and Lore: The Southern Districts*. Fleischmanns, NY: Purple Mountain Press, 2003.

Podskoch, Martin. *Adirondack 102 Club: Your Passport and Guide to the North Country*. Utica, NY: North Country Books, 2014.

___ "Query Form For The United States And Its Territories." Accessed March 23, 2021. https://geonames.usgs.gov/apex/f?p=138:1:::::.

Rajs, Jake. *The Hudson River*. New York. NY: The Monacelli Press, Inc., 1995.

Roosevelt, Theodore and H. D. Minot. *The Summer Birds of the Adirondacks in Franklin County, N. Y.* Sagamore Hill National Historic Site. https://www.theodorerooseveltcenter.org/Research/Digital-Library/Record?libID=o284478. Theodore Roosevelt Digital Library. Dickinson State University.

Rosevear, Francis B. and Barbara McMartin. *Colvin in the Adirondacks: A Chronology and Index: Research Source for Colvin's Published and Unpublished Works*. Utica, NY: North Country Books, 1992.

Schaefer, Paul, ed. *Adirondack Exploration: Nature Writings of Verplanck Colvin.* Syracuse, NY: Syracuse University Press, 1997.

Schlimmer, Erik. *Among the Cloud Splitters: Place Names of High Peaks Wilderness Area*. Troy, NY: Beechwood Books, 2016.

Schlimmer, Erik. *History Inside the Blue Line: Place Names of the Trans Adirondack Route*. Harpersfield, NY: Beechwood Books, 2014.

Schneider, Paul. *The Adirondacks: A History of America's First Wilderness*. New York: Henry Holt and Company, Inc., 1997.

Scofield, Bruce. *High Peaks of the Northeast: A Peakbagger's Directory and Resource Guide to the Highest Summits in the Northeastern United States*. North Amherst, MA: New England Cartographics, Inc., 1994.

Short, Noelle. "Goodman Mountain: a local tribute to a national hero." Accessed April 24, 2019. https://www.tupperlake.com/blog/2015/02/goodman-mountain-local-tribute-national-hero.

Spafford, Horatio Gates. *A Gazetteer of the State of New-York*. Albany, NY: H.C. Southwick, 1813. Accessed May 5, 2021. https://archive.org/details/gazetteerofstate01spaf.

Street, Alfred B. *The Indian Pass*. Accessed January 26, 2020. archive.org/details/indianpass00strerich/page/n5/mode/2up.

Sulavik, Stephen B. *Adirondack: Of Indians and Mountains 1535-1838*. Fleischmanns, NY: Purple Mountain Press, 2007.

Sylvester, Nathaniel Bartlett. *Northern New York and the Adirondack Wilderness*. Troy, NY: William H. Young, 1877.

Tefft, Tim, ed. *Of the Summits, of the Forests*. Morrisonville, NY: Adirondack 46ers, 1991.

Timm, Ruth. *Life in the Adirondacks*. Utica, NY: Pyramid Publishing, Inc., 2007.

___*Trails: Marcy & Skylight*, directed by Martin Paris. (2004; Lake Placid, NY: Adirondack Trails), DVD.

___"In Tribute to VERPLANCK COLVIN 1847-1920 Land Surveyor, Founder, and Champion of the New

York State Forest Preserve and the Adirondack Park Remembered by his friends and admirers on the Centennial of the Adirondack Park-May 20, 1992." Accessed May 21, 2021. http://www.colvincrew.org/core/wp-content/uploads/RecoveryNo.-12.pdf.

Van Dyke, Henry. *Little Rivers*. Accessed April 25, 2021. https://www.sapili.org/english/little-rivers-by-henry-van-dyke.

Wade-Keszey, Dale. *Tributaries: A Lazy Academic's Look at Some Streams, Creeks and Kills Around Schenectady Way*. Schenectady, NY: Vincy's Printing, 2019.

Wadsworth, Bruce. *An Adirondack Sampler: Day Hikes for All Seasons*. Lake George, NY: Adirondack Mountain Club, 1979.

Wallace, Edwin R. *Descriptive guide to the Adirondacks: land of the thousand lakes and to Saratoga Springs; Schroon Lake; lakes Luzerne, George, and Champlain; the Ausable chasm; Massena Springs; and Trenton Falls*. Syracuse, N.Y., W. Gill, 1894. Accessed July 29, 2014. https://archive.org/details/descriptiveguide00walluoft.

Wanner, Marc. "Historic Saranac Lake: Moose Pond." Accessed May 5, 2021. https://localwiki.org/hsl/Moose_Pond.

Webb, Nina H. *Footsteps Through the Adirondacks: The Verplanck Colvin Story*. Utica, NY: North Country Books, 1996.

Weber, Sandra. *Mount Marcy: The High Peak of New York*. Fleischmanns, NY: Purple Mountain Press, Ltd., 2001.

Weber, Sandra. *The Finest Square Mile: Mount Jo and Heart Lake*. Fleischmanns, NY: Purple Mountain Press, Ltd., 1998.

Weber, Sandra. *The Lure of Esther Mountain: Matriarch of the Adirondack High Peaks*. Fleischmanns, NY: Purple Mountain Press, Ltd., 1995.

White, William Chapman. *Adirondack Country*. Syracuse, NY: Syracuse University Press, 1985.

ABOUT THE AUTHOR

Robert (Bob) Lawrence, a Watertown (NY) native, has had a lifetime love for history and the Adirondacks, starting when his parents and grandparents took his sisters and him on trips and excursions throughout the Adirondacks.

While attending Jefferson Community College in Watertown, New York, he helped to organize and guide hiking and canoe trips within the Blue Line for other students to partake in and enjoy.

As a teacher at the elementary and middle schools in the Guilderland Central School District, he helped organize environmental and hiking activities for students inside and outside the Adirondack Park.

After retiring as a teacher in Guilderland, he became a lecturer in Early Childhood and Childhood Education at the State University of New York at Cortland.

Bob received his A.A. from Jefferson Community College, Watertown, (NY), B.A. History from the State University College at Oswego (NY), and an M.S. Reading Education from the State University of New York at Albany.

He also has published several articles on the United States Space Program as the Education Editor for *Space Launch News*. This publication was distributed to spectators at each space shuttle viewing in Florida. Also, he published one book entitled *Sailor of the Stars*, an astronaut teaching simulation for teachers in the classroom. He was one of the editors for *Canadian Studies: A Syllabus and Resource Guide for Elementary and Junior High Teachers.*

He currently resides in Southern Saratoga County (NY) with his wife, Carol Ann, and their wire-haired dachshund, Adirondack, Adi for short. Whenever they can, they spend time in the Adirondacks, enjoying all it has to offer. It is like a second home.

ROBERT C. LAWRENCE, *photo by Gary Garavuso*